Impairment, Disability and Handicap

Impairment, Disability and Handicap
A multi-disciplinary view

Edited by

DENNIS LEES and
STELLA SHAW

Published for the
Social Science Research Council
by
HEINEMANN EDUCATIONAL BOOKS · LONDON

Heinemann Educational Books Ltd
LONDON EDINBURGH MELBOURNE AUCKLAND
HONG KONG SINGAPORE KUALA LUMPUR
IBADAN NAIROBI JOHANNESBURG
LUSAKA NEW DELHI

ISBN 0 435 82530 5

Published by Heinemann Educational Books Ltd,
48 Charles Street, London W1X 8AH
Printed in Great Britain by
Morrison & Gibb Ltd, London and Edinburgh

Preface

This book represents the outcome of a conference sponsored by the Social Science Research Council on 'The Cost of Human Impairment', which took place in March 1973. The conference was made up of a small group of people, distinguished and expert, but who normally did not talk to each other or read each other's work. Differences in intellectual tradition and jargon might have been expected to hamper communication severely, and it was clearly not going to be easy, in a mere couple of days, for useful discussion to emerge.

But, remarkably, it did. The conference was an enormous success. If the resulting book is half as good, most of those involved will be more than satisfied.

The papers were not a survey of the field, if only because there was no field to survey. Indeed, the origins of the conference lay in an uncertain awareness of a growing number of people in different disciplines working on similar problems. They include lawyers, sociologists, social administrators, epidemiologists, psychologists, doctors and medical administrators, engineers (of several varieties), civil servants, perhaps others not yet discovered, and, of course, economists, who are accustomed to poking their noses into everybody's business. So we had to find out what the field was, define some boundaries and make a start on a map of the territory. To cast the notion of 'impairment' too wide would be merely to talk about the state of the world, so we tried to evolve a more limited vision that at the same time took in the notions of 'disability' and 'handicap'. Hence the title of the volume.

A word on dramatis personae is necessary. Dennis Lees acted as programme chairman and records his gratitude to Professors Harry Street and Roy Parker and Dr J P Bull, who represented law, social administration and medicine respectively on the programme committee. Stella Shaw, who also contributes the introductory chapter, was conference secretary. Professor Matthews chaired the opening session of the conference and Alan Williams of York University kindly acted as chairman therefore. Nottingham University was host and the sun shone.

Finally Dennis Lees and Stella Shaw took on the job of editing the papers for publication, and with splendid co-operation from the contributors to the conference, they have done their best.

R. C. O. Matthews
Chairman
Social Science Research Council

Dennis Lees
Professor of Industrial
Economics
Nottingham University

Contents

Notes on contributors

R. L. *Akehurst* is a Lecturer in Economics at Lancaster University. Before joining that university he was Research Fellow at the University of York, working on problems of Industrial Hygiene.

A. J. *Culyer* is Assistant Director of the Institute of Social and Economic Research and a Senior Lecturer in the Department of Economics and Related Studies at the University of York. He is the research director of a programme of economic studies in health care at York.

R. F. F. *Dawson* joined the Road Research Laboratory in 1958, where he has worked on a number of aspects of the economics of traffic and safety. He was previously with BOAC and the Oxford University Institute of Statistics.

Neil Doherty is a Stewart-Wrightson Research Fellow in the Department of Industrial Economics, University of Nottingham. His research interests include compensation for personal injury.

Karen Dunnell is a sociologist and lecturer in the Department of Clinical Epidemiology and Social Medicine at St Thomas's Hospital, London. Before joining St Thomas's she worked for four years at the Institute for Social Studies in Medical Care.

Jessie Garrad, a psychologist and medical social worker, has worked with the Medical Research Council and lectured at St Thomas's Hospital Medical School. She is now a lecturer in the Social Sciences Faculty of Bristol University.

Jacqueline Grad de Alarcon has been sociologist to the Medical Research Council Social Psychiatry Unit 1954–59, and MRC Clinical Psychiatry Unit since 1959. Major research interest is in the evaluation of community psychiatric services and effect of these on the families of the mentally handicapped and mentally ill.

D. R. *Harris* is Deputy-Director of the SSRC Centre for Socio-Legal Studies at Wolfson College, Oxford.

Lorely Ide trained in physiotherapy and ergonomics and worked as a research assistant in the Department of Clinical Epidemiology and Social Medicine, St Thomas's Hospital, London.

Dennis Lees is Professor of Industrial Economics at the University of Nottingham. He is Chairman of the National Insurance Advisory Committee and the Industrial Injuries Advisory Council, and member of the Chief Scientist's Research Committee, Department of Health and Social Security. His current research interest is economic aspects of personal injury.

Rachel Rosser spent five years in general medicine before becoming a psychiatrist. Two of these years were spent in the Department of Medicine at Guy's Hospital investigating the application of operational research to the evaluation of medical care. She continues to have a particular interest in the measurement of the effectiveness of different techniques and systems of treatment.

Peter Sainsbury has been Director of the Medical Research Council's Clinical Psychiatry Unit at Graylingwell Hospital, Chichester, since 1957. A major research interest of the unit is the evaluation of psychiatric services.

Stella Shaw was Secretary to the SSRC's Sociology and Social Administration Committee.

Vincent Watts specializes in the design and implementation of information systems. Recently he has been applying to social institutions the experience he gained as a chartered accountant and in operational research. Three years working with the Police Scientific Development Branch of the Home Office on the development of output measures for the police, and in particular the CID, were followed by two years working with the Department of Health Operational Research Unit.

Introduction

The papers which make up the bulk of this book were written as contributions to a small working conference sponsored by the Social Science Research Council to discuss 'The Cost of Human Impairment'.[1] The decision to hold such a meeting was in itself an interesting and rather surprising one, since although the subject is one in which a great many people express interest, it is also one which inspires little actual research or participation in serious public discussion. Understandably, most are made wary by the considerable challenges posed at many levels, including philosophical and methodological, by attempts to place money values on human impairment, disability and suffering.

Rationale for the conference

Nevertheless, those people who have engaged in studies of social policy and those who actually have to take responsibility for resource allocation, invariably find themselves facing the problems inherent in a situation of finite resources for which there is almost infinite demand; how much to allocate, and to what purposes, in order to achieve maximum results, and what criteria to use as the basis for these decisions? The identification and measurement of the costs of impairment are at the hub of these problems.

Apart from the general delicacy surrounding the subject matter of this meeting, there was, and still is to a large extent, a further barrier to progress in this field. This is the divergency of interests of the people who actually have daily contact with impairment and disability—doctors, lawyers, social workers, employers, families, the individuals themselves—whose practical approaches have in turn to be reconciled to the more academic ones of economists, medical and legal research workers, socio-

---

[1] Held at Rutland Hall, University of Nottingham, on 21–23 March 1973. For list of participants see Appendix B.

logists, psychologists and social administrators. This is, of course, a common problem for much research in the social sciences, but it appears in an acute form in this context, where divergency may amount to clash of interests, due to the frequently differing objectives of each of these groups.

All this is by way of explaining the background to the SSRC's rather timid toe dipped into these particular difficult waters. This background is relevant only in so far as it provides the framework for the meeting itself, which drew on representatives of the groups with interests in the field, notably economists, doctors, lawyers, social administrators and administrators in the health and welfare services, and provides a framework for the differences and the perhaps surprising points of agreement between them which emerged during the discussions.

Policy relevance

Growing public concern with the prevalence of disability and its social and economic consequences in the UK has been reflected through numerous measures over the past few years, the most basic of which have been attempts to assess the incidence of disability in the community at large through surveys. Probably the best known of these is the survey carried out by Amelia Harris (OPCS), which is the data baseline for much subsequent work.

For the purposes of the conference the Department of Health and Social Security provided a background paper (page 173) summing up in convenient form available information on numbers, degrees, causes and costs of impairment. Depending on the definition of 'impairment' and 'disabled', it is estimated that approximately 1 person in 13 aged 16 or over, or 78 per 1,000, has some physical, mental or sensory impairment which to a greater or lesser extent reduces their functional ability. Significantly, the vast majority of those in the severely handicapped category are aged 65 and over.

Estimation of the costs of disablement, as distinguished from those associated with the short-term sick, old people, the unemployed and other groups which tend to be heavy users of the health and welfare services, is not easy, since available figures for many benefits, notably sickness and supplementary benefits, do not distinguish between user-groups.

Nevertheless, the DHSS figures show that, for example, industrial disablement pensions, themselves payable to only a small fraction of the 1½ million disabled, cost £71m a year; the recently introduced invalidity pension (payable after more than 28 weeks of sickness) costs £91m a year; estimates for the eventual annual cost of the attendance allowance for disabled people requiring constant care are around £45m. Direct cash payments of this kind are, of course, only the tip of the huge iceberg of supporting services of all kinds, which together add up to a total annual sum the size of which nobody, at our conference at any rate, was prepared to hazard a guess. And, no matter what final figure one choses to put on this, evidence comes in almost daily that it is clearly not enough, or is not being deployed in the most effective way, since the disabled are perhaps more consistently represented in the ranks of the economically and socially disadvantaged in this country than any other single group.

This illustrates one aspect of the numerous ambiguities and contradictions which surround attitudes to disablement, which recurred constantly at our meeting. These conflicts are not often made explicit, as, like most moral dilemmas, they are embarrassing and particularly hard to resolve and hence preferably ignored. On the one hand, social values are, generally speaking, liberally inclined and public recognition of, and sympathy towards, disablement and its attendant difficulties is high. This has been seen in recent parliamentary and government activity, with the passing of the Chronically Sick and Disabled Persons Act (1970), and is particularly noticeable in the press and other mass media, where cases like the thalidomide children and less spectacular examples of distress have widespread appeal. At the same time those involved—parliament, national and local government, press, television and taxpayers—are equally concerned with the cost of public expenditure, and voters tend to record their views by stolidly rejecting at all levels those administrations which increase their taxes and rates to 'unacceptable' levels.

Examples of the ambivalent and often contradictory attitudes expressed in these matters are found in the field of accident prevention and avoidance, where one government agency will spend a small fortune rescuing a single mountaineer or lost sailor, whilst another cavils at the expenditure necessary to abolish level crossings and to install crash barriers on motorways. It seems clear that people find it more acceptable to incur expendi-

ture on saving lives and disability if it is a question of instant
reaction to a specific emergency, in which case the cost is rarely
counted, rather than long-term calculation of pros and cons and
resource allocation.

Problem formulation

It was interesting to find that this kind of general ambiguity was
to some extent reflected at our meeting, when participants found
themselves from the outset tending to confuse the positive and
normative aspects of the subject under discussion and frequently
arguing on factual matters from the basis of what ought to be
done. There was a secondary form of ambiguity which bedevilled
the conference even at the planning stage; this problem of
definition of terms should be made explicit at the outset. When
we first encountered it this seemed no more than a minor difficulty, which could be resolved in Humpty Dumpty fashion by
people defining and using the words 'impairment', 'disability'
and 'handicap' as they pleased. We don't want to waste time
arguing over terminology, we said; it doesn't matter, if Professor
X uses the terms interchangeably while Dr Y attaches specific
meanings to each one, so long as we know they are doing this.
However, it transpired that these definitions can be very important, and, indeed, reflect one of the most fundamental conceptual
differences of approach to the whole problem of disability that
emerged at the conference. This was seen most clearly in the
conference papers by Doherty and Lees (page 56), Culyer (page
17) and Garrad (page 141). Doherty, Lees and Culyer, writing from
the traditional economists' viewpoint, were able to treat impairment, disability and handicap as one and the same thing, since
the economist is dealing with physical impairment as a general
class of effects which give rise to those costs which are the real
focus of his interest, and can therefore ignore relatively minor
(to him) differences in physical condition. Garrad's study, which
was aimed at an eventual assessment of the provision of health
and social services, required a precise measurement of the kinds
of physical condition which would necessitate different kinds of
help. For this sort of fine-grained work which is used to classify
individual cases rather than broad classes, the question of functional ability to perform different tasks is crucial. Hence her
separation into two distinct categories: *impairment*, 'an anatomical,

pathological or psychological disorder which may be described in diagnostic or symptomatic terms' which 'may cause or be associated with disability so that while every disabled person has an impairment, not all people with impairments are necessarily disabled'—i.e. independence can be maintained (page 142); *disability*, 'limitation of performance in one or more activities which are generally accepted as essential basic components of daily living' (page 142)—i.e. it entails some degree of dependence.

Problems of definition and classification recurred fairly regularly throughout our discussions, and in many different contexts. For example, lawyers and economists involved with the legal mechanics of compensation restrict their attention almost exclusively to accident-induced impairment and disability since it is only in these cases that blame for the accident can be apportioned and the legal system brought into play. Doctors dealing with physical disablement, on the other hand, can make no such initial distinction between causes, but must be prepared to treat people as patients on the basis of the effect manifested in the organism.

It transpired that even definitions according to physical defects or ostensible functional impairment are not the whole answer, since these do not produce the same behavioural effects in different people. Even bearing in mind that independence for physically disabled people with any major functional impairment can only be bought at the cost of fairly heavy investment in special equipment (especially for transport), household adaptations and support services of various kinds, it is noticeable that some people confined to wheelchairs succeed in working and maintaining a high degree of independence whilst others require constant nursing care. Disability is therefore to some extent self-defined, in that (within limits) individuals may or may not accept the role of 'invalid' to which their physical condition entitles them; the existence of this kind of self-definition has been confirmed by survey work, where people checking back on respondents declaring themselves non-impaired in a questionnaire have found obvious impairment. Although this may seem to be a case of semantic nicety, it can have a very practical bearing on the actual cost of impairment, since, clearly, the more people can be given some incentive to reject the invalid role and maintain independence, the less will be their overall support cost.

Finally, we have to ask at what point impairment alone can really be in any way treated as disablement. Everybody is impaired, to the extent that some people are less intelligent or beautiful than others, or have warts or are fat, but how far can or should this be compensated?

Assessing the costs of impairment and disability

The tendency to blur the lines between the positive and normative aspects of costing impairment and disability was, understandably, at its most marked whenever we moved away from the general to the particular. General conceptual papers on the economist's approach to impairment or on the costs of the prevention, alleviation and treatment of disability led to discussion of the conceptual or methodological problems inherent in these exercises. Identification of these costs is, after all, largely a matter of disentangling them from a general welter of similar information relating to other categories of people, and putting them neatly into pigeon-holes, as Dr Dawson does in his paper on 'The Cost of Human Impairment from Road Accidents' (page 94), which also reflects both the highly developed state of costing on accident avoidance and of public acceptance of objective evaluation of the cost of lives in these circumstances.

A second paper on the identification of costs (R. L. Akehurst, 'Regulating the use of Asbestos', page 81), however, revealed further problematic considerations. On the cost side, Akehurst points out that the possibility of avoiding costs through abandoning asbestos is not promising. The existing large stock of asbestos in circulation cannot be withdrawn and, even if a substitute were possible, it might itself produce after-effects, be expensive to develop and less efficient in use. In the case of asbestosis, the 'paternalistic' issue of who should take decisions arises because the effects of inhalation of asbestos dust are not seen for many years, workers have continued to expose themselves to the risk in the hope that it won't happen to them, and the question has to be put whether or not this should be permitted.

Few people would object to these exercises and most would think them useful. However, as soon as discussion turns to the question of who bears these costs—the individual, the family, the community—it is more difficult to keep within the boundaries of 'is'. Indeed, since the conference was inspired by the growing need to probe into the 'ought' side of these questions, there was no reason why we *should* have kept to the factual matters. The real problem was, however, that although several people knew that they could not altogether accept the economists' approach to the questions of who should pay, and how much, they could not profess any real alternatives; and the economists themselves do not have any firm answers to the question of who should receive the benefits. The classic economists' answer to questions involving choice and rationing is the pricing system which, in layman's terms, would mean that the choices between a whole range of alternatives and services, such as hospital or home care, or benefits payable in a lump sum or periodic payments, would be determined by peoples' willingness and ability to agree and pay a price for these alternatives. This method would satisfy both those who seek efficient resource allocation on economic grounds and those who object to the 'paternalistic' attitudes often seen in those who make decisions on the treatment of disabled people.

There are several objections to this approach; it would rely on the availability of adequate information as well as a capacity to understand, and would require a standardization of costing procedures to enable real comparison to be made between alternatives and different parts of the system; for example, at present accident prevention is based on the full social cost of accidents, whilst care systems are calculated on direct cost accounting. Also, income is unequally distributed and impairment, handicap and disability often reduce ability to pay still further.

Another, more fundamental question is who would choose between available alternatives, once the decision was removed from the hands of the doctor or social workers. Would the patient decide what price he would pay to be looked after at home rather than in hospital? This might be neither realistic nor just, since there is always the possibility that the disabled person is not competent, because of their physical or mental condition, to make such a decision. Doctors could hardly be expected to take responsibility for the physical condition of those patients who chose their own environment, perhaps in the face of medical indications to the contrary. Or, perhaps most important, the disabled person's decision to be treated at home might clash with the wishes of his or her own family.

Home or hospital care-case studies

Some light on these issues was cast by the research reports from

Dunnell and Sainsbury (pages 106 and 123), both of whom have attempted to assess the relative costs and satisfactions given to two quite different kinds of patients (polio victims and mentally sick) by home care and hospital care. Their results are significant and pertinent to the concrete problems of coping with disabled people, as opposed to the general intellectual problems of disablement and impairment.

Both studies in fact shift the emphasis away from the disabled individual where interest tends to concentrate, and put the focus on their families, and the impact of disability on them. In general it is much cheaper to maintain and treat a disabled person in their own home than in a hospital (£10 per week as against £70 per week). Against this must be put the quality of care received at home (which may not be as good as that in a hospital), the type of treatment that may be needed (Dunnell's study showed that responants still require hospital back-up treatment) and the possible conflict of interest within the family. Even where a family actively wishes to care for a disabled member at home, there is the question of who should receive and/or spend the money—the disabled person or the one, almost invariably a woman, who bears the burden of the work.

Reverting briefly to the question of costing, it should be noted that home care is at present heavily subsidized by the time and work of women; if they were to be paid even the lowest hospital rates, the comparative figures for home and hospital care would require radical revision. Furthermore, in the United States at least, the Women's Liberation movement is leading women to cut off this kind of care even though this may be done inadvertently by encouraging women to move out of the home into work. The question could conceivably resolve itself with hospital becoming the only available place for the majority of disabled people. However, this is still at present the remotest possibility, since women are still subjected to tremendous social pressures to adopt and maintain the caring role, and only the most toughminded are prepared to make any stand even on less emotional issues than caring for disabled relatives.

Apart from the basic problem of sorting out and attempting to weight the costs and benefits of home and hospital care, there is the related issue of assessing the effectiveness of hospital care itself. An attempt to devise a method for comparing different hospitals was presented at the conference by Dr Rosser and

Dr Watts, whose concern in their study described in their paper 'The development of a classification of the symptoms of sickness and its use to measure the output of a hospital' (page 157) was to devise a method for classifying degrees of disability and distress, and the effectiveness of the hospital in relieving different conditions. There are, of course, methodological objections to this procedure. If the Rosser/Watts index were to be used to make judgments about individual cases or to evaluate the comparative performance of different hospitals, might there not be a possibility that hospitals would try to fill their beds with minor cases showing a high likelihood of improvement, thus boosting their 'success' rate? There is, indeed, a fair body of evidence[1] which shows that voluntary hospitals indulged in this kind of practice in pre-National Health days when they had to compete with each other to attract funds. Second, there is the question of deployment of resources, and whether they really are liberated by sending people out of hospital; the actual hospital services are still required intermittently, and, if people require constant care, this can in fact create duplication of care services in hospital and home. Third, who should get the money; the patient may gain by being at home, whilst his family is less satisfied and requires compensation for loss of satisfaction. Also, it has been found that disabled people need the actual skills of doctors and nurses, and that they can accept the role and status of patient from professionals when it is unacceptable from members of their families. Nevertheless the Rosser/Watts approach is an important step in the development of hospital care assessment and has the advantage over many other methods of allowing for changes over time to be discerned.

Needless to say, we were not able to arrive at any precise solutions to these kinds of problems. The best that can be done at present is to pose the questions, and recognize that the answers cannot be absolute but only relative to particular cases and needs. Many disabled people could in fact be cared for at home to the mutual satisfaction of patient and family, providing there were adequate support services for the family and some respite available for both when necessary—for example, fairly regular 'holidays' in hospital to give the family a rest.

---

[1] B. Abel Smith (with the assistance of R. Pinker), *The Hospitals*, 1800–1948: A study in Social Administration in England and Wales, London, Heinemann, 1964.

Compensation

Implicit in all our discussions of caring for disabled people is the assumption that it is unjust to allow them to bear alone the losses and damages they have incurred—indeed this notion of compensating for disadvantages is perhaps the most widely accepted in this country today even though, as has already been noted, it may be applied inconsistently and does not stand up to logical analysis. We should also note that the growth of compensation is in fact constantly creating pressure for more compensation.

We noted earlier that everyone is impaired, to a greater or less extent, but so far we lack any real policy or mechanism for deciding what should be compensated or for making any re-assessments over time of conditions for which people are receiving compensation; the introduction of such a mechanism could itself create an incentive to people to delay improvement until after a re-assessment had taken place. A senior civil servant has already voiced his own personal nightmare of a time when one half of the country is being compensated by the other half. Nevertheless, we do have an extensive and complex system of compensation, which takes many forms and operates chiefly through the state, the insurance world and the courts and we are constantly searching to improve these mechanisms in a way which will minimize the cost to individuals and the community, whilst distributing them as equitably as possible.

These compensation mechanisms, with their legal and economic concommitants, were a second focal point for the conference, and it was this aspect of impairment which showed itself to be most amenable to the introduction of concrete changes. The appointment of a Royal Commission on Civil Liability and Compensation for personal injury, which was announced as we were finalizing our plans for the conference, confirms the general view that the legal system is at least ripe for re-appraisal, if not for faily fundamental change. This system, which is described in some detail in the papers by Harris (page 30) and Doherty and Lees (page 56) is based on the principle of tort on which our legal mechanisms currently rest, i.e. finding someone to blame who can be made to pay for an accident. It is a notion which tends to confuse the purposes of compensation for damage, since the underlying idea and eventual result seems to be more that of punishing the 'guilty' than compensating the victim for loss and damage. For example, a survey quoted by Harris (page 32) of accident victims in 1967–68 revealed that fewer than half the respondents who sustained injuries resulting in more than 6 weeks absence from work made successful claims for damages, because of the considerable difficulty which is always experienced of establishing negligence on the part of the defendants. Of those who were successful, only four-fifths recovered more than their actual financial losses, and were consequently compensated in some way for the damages they sustained. Thus it could be claimed that the greatest beneficiaries from the tort system are the legal and medical professions, since their expenses form a large part of the very high costs of the system. It is also anomalous since it means that we accept a situation in which the same degree of functional disability can be handsomely compensated in one man whilst another has to join the supplementary benefits queue.

Apart from this basic principle, the present mechanisms for calculating loss and damage are open to criticism, particularly the failure of courts to use actuarial methods for calculating loss and damage, as proposed by the Law Commission. Further, the 'lump sum' method means that compensation is estimated on prognostications for the future, which may be wrong, with the result that compensation is inappropriate.

The tort system is not, however, entirely without its defenders, who argue that it may not be perfect but is preferable to known alternatives, such as the introduction of overall compensation irrespective of fault. Under this, all victims would be compensated regardless of who was to blame for their misfortune and this would, it is claimed, mean both that much more money would have to be found and that individuals would actually receive smaller sums—the familiar argument of more means less. Perhaps the most telling argument in favour of retaining an element of blame is that this does in fact have some deterrent effect. For example, the legal liability of firms for industrial accidents has led to improved safety measures and a reduction in accidents, whilst certain types of high-powered sports cars have been virtually priced out of the insurance market, due to their propensity to be involved in expensive accidents. Tort can therefore be said to provide an incentive to avoid causing damage and, in this sense, is efficient in economic terms.

In fact, there is no necessary connection at all between the two sides of compensation, and it should be quite possible to separate the question of payment for the costs of impairment from compensation for victims. Theoretically, all accident victims could be compensated irrespective of fault, but recovery of costs could be undertaken on the basis of fault, thus retaining the disincentive element although this may lead to large costs in time and trouble. Nevertheless, the consensus opinion at the conference was heavily in favour of a move to this kind of system.

The determination of the amount of compensation would then have to be carried out by another, presumably non-legal, agency which would have to cope with a different set of problems not related in any way to the causes of accidents. One obvious problem would be whether compensation should take account of the circumstances of the victim, i.e. whether rich and poor should be compensated equally. The economists answer to this would be that individuals should set a value on their own health, and pay according to the returns they desired; in practice this would mean that society would set norms, and individuals could go above these by paying more. Even using this as a broad guideline there would still be difficulties to resolve, as people's requirements for compensation would vary according to the kind of impairment incurred; no amount of money would, presumably, really compensate anyone for quadraplegia, whereas most people could estimate fairly well what a broken leg would cost them in terms of lost income, etc. Again, such an agency might perhaps reconsider the built-in assumption that there should be compensation for psychic disturbance and loss, which is an extremely difficult factor to estimate. In the USSR, for example, only pecuniary loss can be compensated, and this at least sets all victims on a more equal footing.

The decision process

By the end of our two days of discussion it had become apparent that the one factor which had not been tackled openly was the political one. Little mention was made of the political context within which the choices and decisions concerning impairment and disability are made, or, indeed, of who takes these decisions. To some extent this was predetermined by the need to focus the conference on a relatively limited topic, but the general reluctance to discuss the political realities was nevertheless surprising, in view of the enormous sums of money which change hands in the process of the prevention, treatment, alleviation and compensation of disablement, with which many of the people present were actively concerned. For example community care is currently a fashionable concept, and there is a lot of pressure for home care and treatment of various kinds of long-term illness. This appears to be the result of administrative decisions, taken on the basis of crude cost calculations without taking into account the kinds of considerations already discussed above. Little political debate has taken place, and the switch in emphasis from hospital to home care has taken place without provoking public discussion of the kind generated by so many recent changes in, for example, the educational system. No political party has embraced these issues with the fervour which surrounded debates on the introduction of comprehensive education or the abandonment of free milk. Education is, of course, an area where politicians are subject to powerful lobbying from the consumers—or rather, their parents—and, although no politician wishes to appear sufficiently illiberal as to cast doubt on the generally held notion that the disabled must be cared for, few wish to actually challenge any move aimed directly at cutting these costs—not even to the extent of examining them closely. Other factors at work include the general layman's reluctance to question decisions which appear to be based on the clinical judgment of the medical profession.

At present the small but highly active pressure groups which have grown up to press the case for greater financial support for disabled people seem generally content to agitate for an overall increase in funds allocated to the purpose, rather than for any fundamental re-examination of the thinking behind the spending. This is, again, easily understood, since they are breaking new ground so far as disablement is concerned and their priorities lie with getting a larger cake rather than worrying about the recipe and ingredients.

Only one area of the cost of human impairment is currently under public review, that of compensation for physical damage due to accident, and even here it appears that the attention of the Royal Commission will be confined largely to the appropriateness of tort as a basis for deciding whether or not compensation is due. It will not, for example, consider whether such compensation should be extended to severe congenital abnormalities. The decision to mount such a Royal Commission was a political one

as was the definition of its terms of reference, and was the outcome of a single accident with a new drug rather than of any
deliberate recognition that the present system might be inefficient,
unjust and outmoded.

It may well be that this apparent lack of a public interest in and
debate over the most desirable measures for coping with problems
arising from serious impairment and disability is an expression of
the fundamental conflict between two major factors which policy
must take into account. These are the need to minimize the
overall cost of impairment, and the wish to distribute those costs
equally among the population. The first consideration derives
from hard-headed financial and economic considerations, and the
second from the implicit social judgment that the troubles of
those who have been treated 'unfairly' by circumstances should,
as far as possible, be shared by the community.

The clash between the value judgment and the economic issues
manifests itself in several ways. Economics demands that we
minimize costs by encouraging measures by both individuals and
the community that will prevent impairment and disability; that
we limit their extent where prevention is unavoidable; and that we
minimize the consequences of disability and the suffering it causes,
partly through offering incentives to people to achieve the
maximum independance their physical condition will allow, and
partly by providing support through financial compensation and
services.

These measures are, in fact, at odds with the principle of
equity, which implies that all sufferers should receive full compensation for their disabilities, without acknowledging that such
compensation might actually have a disincentive effect at both
the collective and individual levels.

It seems highly likely that we will continue to muddle along
in our policies, swayed first by economic considerations and
then by our values, unless these issues are made explicit and
subjected to public scrutiny.

Although of course it may be that the protagonists in the
debates which do take place are fully aware of this dilemma, and
prefer it to remain hidden and unresolved rather than risk a
possible change in public attitudes which could be unfavourable
to their own approach.

1

GENERAL ISSUES

Introduction

The three chapters in this section deal with the general issues underlying the economic and legal approaches to the problems of attempting to cost impairment and disability, and to compensate people who suffer physical damage.

The first chapter, by Culyer, is aimed at the layman in economics, particularly people from other disciplines and professions who may be trying to apply unfamiliar concepts to familiar problems of resource allocation. The author goes into the rationale behind the economists' approach—the philosophical underpinning, the place of values in the economists' calculations, the chief factors taken into account in cost-benefit analysis—and illustrates the scope and limitations of this approach as a basis for making decisions about the treatment of individual disabled people.

Don Harris gives a straightforward account of the present legal system for compensation of physical damage through accidents. He concentrates on the principle of 'tort', or 'fault', which is the foundation stone of legal compensation in this country.

The third chapter in this group, by Doherty and Lees, straddles both the economic and the legal approaches to impairment and compensation. It is, indeed, aimed at elucidating the economic basis, or lack of it, of current processes for calculating and awarding damages, and consequently links together the themes of the two preceding papers.

1 Economics, Social Policy and Disability

A. J. CULYER

An ethical basis in economics

Economists, like most other social scientists, seek to identify social policies and general rules for regulating society that are in the 'social interest' rather than those that may be the result either of special pleading on some minority's behalf on the one hand or of the analyst's *personal* political and social values on the other. Although there is some argument both about whether this is desirable and even whether it is possible, I shall take this starting point as given.[3][1]

One needs, of course, to define 'social interest' rather clearly and I hope I do my colleagues no injustice in saying that the adjective 'social' is supposed to mean no more than the total collection of individuals that is taken as constituting a society. In its most extreme form society has been taken to mean *every* individual. Others, however, place restrictions on its scope by, for example, excluding 'foreigners', 'children' the 'insane' and so on, all suitably defined. Conventionally, economists do exclude children and the insane. Practice varies as to how foreigners are treated—some economists are 'multinationalists' and others 'nationalists'. Generally, exclusions beyond these are not admitted. For example it is not customary to exclude 'Jews' or 'Conservatives'.

The notion of 'interest' is unambiguously individualistic. Generally speaking, if an individual (who is not excluded from the definition of 'society') prefers one thing, or course of action, to another, that thing is taken as being in the social interest by virtue of its being in his—provided, of course, that someone else

---

[1] Figures in square brackets refer to references on page 29.

is in no way harmed thereby. The 'social interest' thus becomes identified with the total of all (eligible) individual interests; but not quite all, for again exclusions are commonly made. I may like my bedroom walls pink but you may prefer *mine* to be blue. A strict application of the individualistic principle would require either me to compensate you for the 'harm' I did you by having them pink or for you to compensate me for the harm you did me by requiring me to have them blue. Conventionally, there is a set —usually not very well-defined—of such effects that are excluded on a kind of liberal principle. Thus, if my walls are pink, no matter how offensive you find this knowledge it is 'none of your business' (unless you are my wife). Similarly, I think many of us would exclude some of the benefits that individuals derive from 'illegitimate' activities. We do not, for example, customarily include the thrills experienced by burglars in burgling on the plus side of any attempt to estimate the socially optimum deployment of crime prevention and detection resources. Clearly there is a penumbra of activities here about which there is no convention.[1]

Note at this stage that although certain categories of person and certain objects of desire may be excluded from directly entering what is usually termed the 'social welfare function' that is not to say that they may not be important for social welfare, though in an indirect way. Although, for example, 'children' may not be included in 'society' (i.e. count among those individuals whose welfare, as they see it, is to be counted as being a part of social welfare) the views of *other people*, such as parents, teachers, social workers, friendly strangers, etc., about the well-being of children most certainly do enter in. In jargon, children have no 'internalities' but create very important 'externalities'.

From this basis, the complicated apparatus of welfare economics gets built up. The objective is, of course, to identify changes in policy or the rules of the game used by a society that will lead to an improvement in social welfare. The difficulties that crop up are

---

[1] All the exclusions discussed are exclusions only in *normative* economics. In many *positive* cases one may be interested in predicting the behaviour of infants, wall-painters and criminals, whose *actions* will be affected by their interests as they see them and as they impinge on others. Some of my colleagues would not make any of the exclusions mentioned here. This, however, seems to me to be unnecessarily extreme. Technically, it also implies that the 'Pareto criterion' for an improvement in social welfare as compared with the 'potential Pareto criterion, is rarely, if ever, possible to apply.

very many and the solutions proposed ingenious and not always entirely successful (though frequently they are better than anything else in sight). Some of these difficulties and their proposed solutions are discussed elsewhere in this book. Here I wish just to mention a few fundamental ones.

The revelation of individual values

As expounded so far, a person's interest or welfare has not been quantified. How then, can one know whether his welfare has increased or decreased? The conventional approach is to infer the direction of changes in welfare by *behaviour*. Thus, if two persons voluntarily agree to a particular set of arrangements we infer that their welfare increases on the assumption that only each can know his own welfare and the presumption that he does not seek his own diswelfare. Note this does not imply selfishness. If a person voluntarily gives to a charity, *his* welfare, in our sense, increases —given his interests (unselfish ones), they are being served. A great deal of the analysis of market operations takes place with no stronger a form of measurement than this—ordinal utility, if you like.

But what of changes that increase one person's welfare and at the same time reduce another's? Given the subjectivity of the concept of welfare and its inalienability from the individual, it may appear that little can be said. This would seem disastrous, because many desired objects (from a man's labour to a wheelchair) are customarily owned by some individual, or the state, so that if one person is to improve his welfare he can do so, in these cases, *only* at another's expense. The standard method adopted in western societies for dealing with such cases is to create a situation whereby the potential loser gets adequately compensated for parting with that which he owns whether it be his labour or the wheelchair he (or the firm) owns (or may have just manufactured). This is, of course, the purpose of markets. In the process, some measures of social benefit or cost are revealed. For example, the sum (whether in terms of money or anything else) voluntarily received by the person who gives something up must *at least* compensate him for the loss. It cannot, on our assumptions, be less than the true cost inflicted upon him by the loss. On the other side, the sum paid by the party acquiring whatever it is must be at most the value he places upon having it. Any changes that are voluntarily acceded to (whether via compensation or not) may then be taken as improvements in social welfare. It is not surprising, perhaps, that the manifest flexibility of the voluntary trading process in markets, which automatically reveals the changing valuations of myriad individuals and thrusts upon individuals the costs of each of countless decisions, has seduced many into supposing that the market does this job of cost and benefit revelation either perfectly or more perfectly than alternative institutional forms. An alternative extreme reaction is that where the market reveals individual values badly some alternative (such as government) *must* do it better.

It is true, of course, that many of the most valuable things in life do not get priced and these I will return to later, but even for those that are there are problems. An obvious one is transactions that take place under 'duress' (e.g. compulsory purchases or sales by a monopolist). I do not propose to discuss these in any detail (an approach to them is implicit in our later discussion of unpriced sources of welfare). A less obvious one is that the value revealed for a good is partly dependent upon the quantity one has of whatever it is that one is giving up to acquire it. The various solutions to this problem and the circumstances under which they can be used are too technical to be dealt with in this paper.

Perhaps more obvious, and certainly of great social concern, is the fact that the value one individual reveals for something, *compared with another individual*, depends upon their relative ownership of the numeraire commodity—commonly money. Thus, where uncompensated losses occur, it is not valid to add up the (money value of the) gains to the gainers and the losses to the losers and subtract the latter from the former to see if there is a *net* social gain. Every individual may express a 'correct' value, but it will be a value partly determined by his command over resources in general—by his (human and non-human) wealth. Even if everyone agreed (which they do not) that the distribution of wealth in society were ideal, it would still not follow that the values placed by individuals on entities need be those that society ought to accept, for the weights implied even by an ideal distribution of wealth (whatever 'ideal' may mean here) may not be the ideal weights to use for the specific task in hand. Thus, we may all agree that one man deserved to be four times richer than another but we would not necessarily want to accept that because the maximum sum he would give to acquire an object is four

times the poor man's maximum voluntary payment that he values
it four times as much as the poor man. In truth, we can never
know how much more he values it than the poor man. We can
say, on the one hand, if the poor man owns it and voluntarily sells
it to the rich man that each gains. On the other hand, if we do not
let them trade, or if for some reasons they cannot engage in
voluntary bargaining, we can say that the transfer from the poor
to the rich man is a *potential* improvement if the rich man could
compensate the poor man and still be better off himself. We cannot
tell for sure if it is an *actual* improvement unless compensation
actually takes place, for it is the voluntary payment of actual
compensation that gives us the necessary information that no one
is losing from the transaction.

In applied economics—in cost-benefit analysis for example—it
is conventional to regard a pound lost or gained by a rich man as
of equal value to a pound lost or gained by a poor man. The
implied unitary weighting system is arbitrary but it is convenient.
If society prefers and can (somehow) reveal a different set of
weights, once this set is identified it can be used instead of the
one-for-one set, which should be regarded as no more than
provisional. Cost-benefit analysis is thus concerned only with
potential improvements in social welfare.

Non-revealed and imperfectly revealed social welfare

In practice, as we all know, the market place reveals values in an
imperfect way and frequently fails to reveal them altogether. A
firm must pay a positive wage even to a man who would, for sure,
be otherwise unemployed. The wage will not necessarily correspond very closely to the cost imposed on society by using him
in that job. A beautiful view gets spoiled by a developer but it is
unlikely that the price he paid to the owner of the land also
compensates all those who formerly 'owned' (in a loose sense) the
view. The careless driver may be no more careless than *he* wants
but he may not account for the risks to which he subjects others.
A purely private market in health care cannot allow for the
collective compassion we may all feel for those who cannot afford
the medical care we may feel they should have.[1] Sometimes

---

[1] To my mind, this is the principal reason for having a National Health
Service.

Nature imposes losses on individuals. The losses experienced by a Mongoloid child are evidently revealed extremely imperfectly by any market process.

In these cases we have broadly two problems. First, what costs —or benefits—are involved and what is their size? Secondly, what should we do about them? I shall postpone a discussion of the second question to the next section.

Putting monetary values upon entities that do not normally have them is the aspect of cost-benefit analysis that most taxes the imagination of the analyst and also, unfortunately, is that which most frustrates him as well as raising the suspicions of non-economists. It is, of course, an all pervasive problem in the social policy arena. There is no pat general solution, for there are several social mechanisms by which the values in question may be revealed. It will largely be a matter of judgment as to which mechanism reveals them best. Let me just emphasize two things: (a) the money expenditures incurred in the process of doing something are not necessarily good measures of the *real* costs of the resources thus purchased; (b) non-pecuniary costs are in no way conceptually distinct from any other costs. In either case we may use market data, adjusted market data, data derived from a politico/administrative process, and so on. The kind of choice menu might be illustrated by considering the costs imposed upon an individual by forms of disability about which we shall doubtless hear a lot but, as a preliminary, it will always be necessary to enquire into the meaning of 'disability'.

The ambiguity of the idea of 'disability' springs from its implicit relativity. In the case of an individual whose 'ability' is reduced by some dramatic or traumatic event in his life, one meaning emerges as an obvious one. Thus, in the case of a road accident victim, for example, the disability is the difference between the ability of the person before and after the event. In the case of congenital disability, however, the benchmark for comparison is far less clear. A person with an I.Q. of 130 is not regarded as 'disabled' though he clearly is disabled in the respect of I.Q. compared with a person whose I.Q. is 160. Even a person with lower than average I.Q. is not regarded as disabled or handicapped—unless his I.Q. is very much lower than normal.[1]

---

[1] This example should not be taken as meaning that I have taken extreme sides in the 'nature versus nurture' debate.

Even though it is possible—and efforts in this direction should be encouraged—to devise moderately objective indicators of the severity of disability, it seems that disability and handicap are ultimately subjective concepts. Society, or some sector of society, forms a view as to what a disability is. A handicapped person becomes one who is regarded by society as handicapped. I suspect that the necessary condition that has to be met is that society makes a subjective and informal assessment of the costs imposed by 'circumstances' on a person—the extent to which an impairment reduces an individual's welfare by significantly affecting the options, or life-chances, he faces, where the options are interpreted as *relevant* ones in terms of the environment in which the individual lives. When these costs are 'substantially' higher than the costs imposed on a normal, average or median person by acceptable or at least commonly accepted limitations on his ability, such an individual gets the label 'handicapped'. If this view is correct, it follows that the notion of cost is inherently inseparable from the notion of disability. In defining one the other is defined as well. Let us then consider some of the ways in which these costs—or some of them—may be revealed more objectively.

There are broadly two approaches adopted by economists to such a problem. In practical terms they correspond to looking for empirical evidence in answer to one or two questions:

(*a*) If the individual loses from a disabling event, what is the *minimum* sum he requires to restore his welfare to its original level?

(*b*) If the individual gains from some means of reducing the consequences of a disability he has, what is the *maximum* sum he will pay to receive these means?[1]

These conceptual methods of translating a subjective experience into objective data do not, rather obviously, give the same result

---

[1] The following measure (*b*) is emphasized in the rest of this chapter as being an appropriate measure of the cost imposed *by disability*. However, measure (*a*) is usually the appropriate measure of the cost of 'inputs' used in reducing a person's degree of disability. The market price of an iron lung, for example, is a good indicator of its cost if it is close either to the minimum required to compensate the manufacturer for parting with it or to the minimum price needed to ensure someone else does not purchase it (whichever is the higher).

even though they have the same technical name: 'compensating variations' in wealth. Which measure is the appropriate one clearly depends on the circumstances of the case being considered but a difficulty arises from the clear possibility that measure (*a*) might take on a value that is indefinitely high. Thus, I am not sure that there is any price that would persuade me to let you saw off my (healthy) leg but there is a price, and it is substantially less than my total wealth, that I (if I am legless) would pay for an artificial limb, or even a perfectly functioning leg graft.

The difficulty of one measure possibly approaching infinity is much reduced where the victim has no legal right of redress by considering that the losses felt by a disabled individual have to be compensated voluntarily *by other individuals*. The size of the compensation is more appropriately measured, in such a case, by the maximum sum the rest of society will pay to meet the tragedy. To be sure, this is not a measure of the cost to the disabled person out, since others must lose if he is to be compensated, it is right that their judgment should be the one which counts. The compensation they actually pay may well be less than the loss he feels he has suffered, but for him to insist on receiving still more compensation would mean that while he would gain the rest of society would, in net terms, lose and we have no scientific way of comparing such gains and losses. The further compensation *may* improve social welfare as a whole or it *may not*. We simply cannot tell. The collective judgment as to what should be paid in such cases is properly taken, in my view, by persons with collective responsibility. These may be the officials of charitable organisations or, alternatively, the government, for these are the ways in which collective values get themselves expressed. I do not think there is any obvious way in which even the most inventive cost-benefit analyst could devise a 'shadow-price' for 'collective compassion'. Part of the job of governments is, of course, precisely to give expression to such collective urges. (More strictly, it is part of the job of *democratic* governments.)

In cases where measure (*b*) is appropriate again it is commonly the case that the preferences of members of society in addition to disabled persons need to be accounted for. If society at large derives a benefit from seeing the effects of handicap moderated then society, again through collective agencies, aids the individual by, for example, subsidising medical care and equipment for the handicapped.

In the preventive area, where we are considering measures to reduce the number of disabling events or to moderate the severity of the consequences we are also concerned with measure (*b*). In such cases one is typically dealing with 'statistical' individuals. The question is not 'what will I pay to avoid paraplegia as a possible consequence of an accident on a badly lit and winding road?' but 'what will I pay for a reduction in the *probability* of that event occurring?' Broadly speaking, two approaches to this problem have been adopted by economists. One is to devise experiments to elicit specific answers from 'representative' individuals as to what they would pay. The theory behind this approach is fascinating, but too complex to be gone into here [4]. The alternative is to calculate the losses sustained by a (statistical) individual suffering such a disaster and argue that he would pay *at least* these to avoid such a (statistical) event. In addition, it is common to attempt to calculate what losses would be sustained by the rest of the community as well, as an estimate of what *it* would pay over and above this sum.

Although a fair amount of work has been and is being done which is relevant to the *valuation* of the consequences of disabling events [6] relatively little has, as yet, taken place in the sphere of *measuring* the consequences to be valued. It is, however, obvious (at least to me!) that the operation of an efficient health service and the devising of efficient policies to prevent, treat and assist disability is crucially dependent upon the satisfactory measurement of outcomes (see, Cochrane [2] for an impassioned plea—by an epidemiologist). R. J. Lavers, Alan Williams and I have argued elsewhere [4] the desirability *and feasibility* of output measurement in the health services and Williams, together with his colleague Ken Wright at the University of York, has made substantial progress in the practical measurement of disability among the elderly. Rachel Rosser and Vincent Watts have already made great progress with a related problem in hospitals [7]. Strictly speaking, of course, this output measurement problem—the problem of measuring the observable consequences of policies towards ill-health and disability—is prior to the valuation problem. You have to have something to value. When you cost alternative ways of doing the same thing, you need to be sure that it *is* the same thing. This is an appropriate place at which to emphasise that economists are far from adequately equipped to assess the effectiveness of therapies or to understand fully the physical and social consequences of disability. What they are equipped for is an understanding of the logic of choice. They know the kinds of measures that are needed if sensible choices are to be made. Clearly this is one of the many areas in which society may have much to gain from multidisciplinary collaboration. And perhaps patients (why not call them people?) may get a look-in on the act too, for ultimately it is the kind of output *they* want and the kind of values *they* place on it that is our principal —if not our only—aim.

What should be done about disability?

As far as compensation payments for disability are concerned I think the foregoing invites us to conclude that the appropriateness of any sum should in general be decided by the community in the light of the compassion it feels and what it will sacrifice to give effect to compassion. This is, indeed, the appropriate answer in those cases where individuals do not have prior legal right to compensation for disabling events.

Where individuals have legal rights to compensation, however, things change somewhat. One method, of course, is for individuals to purchase the right to compensation. This is the case in which one insures oneself against risks. The other method is for individuals to be *given* the right to compensation by society. On the one hand, as we have just seen, society might award the right to certain benefits in cash and kind to disabled persons. On the other, society might choose to assign legal liability to individuals who can be identified as 'causing' others to become disabled. It is not clear (to me) precisely according to which criterion damages either are or ought to be evaluated. If the objective is fully to compensate the victim then, in principle, either of the two conceptual measures suggested above are appropriate. It may also be desired, however, that the liability rights be 'limited' according to the other party's 'ability to pay'—as judged by the community. Indeed, we can absolve the party 'at fault' from any obligation to pay at all. We can also arrange compensation procedures so as to affect the behaviour of potential victims and those who directly 'cause' the damage. Since insurance, and the law of tort are both discussed elsewhere in this book, I shall say no more about the problem of getting what might be called an 'efficient' rate of damage. Once again, it seems to me that it is not the business of professional groups to say what the rights should be and how they should be assigned—society must decide this. The difficult matter of *measuring* the costs of disability, as distinct from that of whether they should be compensated, does on the other hand fall clearly into the economic area (not, I hasten to add, *exclusively* in this area) and so does that of how one can affect the probability of disabling events occurring.

I want finally briefly to touch upon the question of mitigating some of the consequences of disability, *not* by paying the disabled person a straight compensatory sum, but by affecting the environment in which he lives and, more specifically, in which he works, so that the consequences of disability become less oppressive.

The characteristic way in which persons suffering from some competitive disadvantage manage to obtain work is by offering their labour at a reduced wage. In this way they 'compensate' the employer for any disadvantage he may be at as a result of their disability. (It is, incidentally, quite easy for laymen to underestimate the disadvantages that employers may face.) In a competitive economy only pecuniary disadvantages that reflected the value of real output losses would need to be overcome in this way but in less competitive situations, non-pecuniary disadvantages too may have to be overcome, such as the colour of one's skin [1].

While there is a sense in which such an outcome (in the competitive case) is efficient, it by no means is likely to be regarded as fair, for although it may be fairer than a system which prevented disabled workers from working at *less than* the going wage for able-bodied workers (which would imply no work and no wages rather than work and low wages), it seems that society desires to *share* these costs of handicap rather than have the handicapped bear them fully themselves. Once again, the extent to which this is done is not a matter solely for the handicapped—the mere fact that they suffer losses does not imply any right for them to thrust them, or even part of them, upon the rest of society—but is a social decision properly taken by socially accountable persons who are more likely to reflect the general wishes of society which is the unit that must ultimately decide what rights the disabled are to be given. Neither, I think, can the *economist* say very much, as a professional, about how far one ought to go. He can, however, contribute some expertise in questions concerning the *methods* to be adopted in increasing the earnings of the disabled.

Indeed, the economics are ignored at the peril of the disabled themselves! Thus it is quite easily seen that a simple 'equal pay' rule, while superficially attractive, would be a disaster. 'Equal pay for work of equal value' (supposing you could measure the value of equal work) would not redistribute any of the costs of disability. Equal pay coupled with an obligatory employment quota for disabled persons would thrust the costs almost entirely on employers, other employees and consumers in ways that would usually be rather hard to measure and not necessarily in the ways we would, as a society, regard as fair.

But there is a variety of ways in which more efficient systems of subsidies could be devised both to the greater benefit of the disabled and at a lesser cost to the rest of society [8]. These are clearly matters, as it seems to me, in which the economist's contribution is absolutely essential—and I suspect that his unsentimentality would be much appreciated by disabled persons themselves.

Conclusions

The general propositions listed below would, I believe, be agreed by my own colleagues in the economics profession.

1. Costs and benefits are ultimately subjective experiences that cannot be alienated from the individual experiencing them.

2. The economic concepts of social cost and benefit are based upon a particular ethical view of society usually described as 'Paretian' which implies, among other things, that improvements in social welfare cannot be identified independently of changes in individuals' welfare and that subjective costs and benefits experienced by different individuals cannot be added or subtracted from one another without further value judgments.

3. However, behaviour frequently *reveals* what these costs and benefits are. Cost-benefit specialists are quite expert at evaluating the likely reliability of these revelations. This means, among other things, that financial data may not be reliable indicators of cost. They should therefore be used with care.

4. Collectively felt costs or benefits are frequently revealed only through collective agencies such as government. In some cases it will remain the case that only accountable public persons should make these evaluations. Indeed they are often the only persons in a position to do so.

5. Assignment of legal rights—such as liability for damages—has important distributional and ethical consequences that are not easily judged using the usual economic paradigm, though *behavioural* (non-ethical) consequences of alternative rights assignments may be. The particular rights that are of interest here are (*a*) the rights of the disabled; (*b*) the rights of others involved directly in the events causing disability; (*c*) the rights of those who may bear additional costs due to the disabling event (e.g. families of disabled persons) and (*d*) the rights of the rest of society (especially its right to give vent to generous instincts).

6. There is substantial scope for experimentation in forms of measurement of disability such as (*a*) to make different disabilities comparable in terms of their severity and (*b*) to provide the basic units to which social assessments (prices or priorities) may be attached.

7. There is substantial scope also for cost-effectiveness studies of the alternative ways of mitigating the consequences of disability (and reducing the net costs to the disabled) which include both direct benefits in cash and kind *and* changes in the work environment.

1. Becker, G. S., *The Economics of Discrimination*, Chicago, University of Chicago Press, 1957

2. Cochrane, A. L., *Effectiveness and Efficiency*, London Nuffield Provincial Hospital Trust, 1972

3. Culyer, A. J., *The Economics of Social Policy*, London, Martin Robertson, 1973

4. Culyer, A. J., Lavers, R. J. and Williams, Alan, 'Social Indicators: Health' in Shonfield, A. and Shaw, S. (Eds), *Social Indicators and Social Policy*, London, Heinemann Educational Books, 1972

5. Jones-Lee, M., 'Valuation of Reduction in Probability of Death by Road Accident', *Journal of Transport Economics and Policy*, Vol. 3, 1969, reprinted in Cooper, M. H. and Culyer, A. J. (Eds), *Health Economics*, London, Penguin Books, 1973

6. Mishan, E. J., *Cost-Benefit Analysis*, London, Allen and Unwin, 1971

7. Rosser, R. and Watts, V., 'The Measurement of Hospital Output' *International Journal of Epidemiology*, Vol 1, 1972

8. Wiseman, J., 'Conceptual Framework for Analysis and Development of Special Work arrangements, with Emphasis on their Social Aims', Experts Group on Special Work Arrangements for Non-Competitive Persons, OECD (mimeo)

2 The Legal System of Compensation for Death and Personal Injury suffered in Accidents

D. R. HARRIS

This chapter deals with the *civil* law on compensation for death and personal injuries; it is not concerned with *criminal* law under which those who cause accidents may be liable to punishment by fine or imprisonment for committing a crime. I have also limited discussion to the strictly legal rules providing for compensation (the word 'legal' is used in the sense of the traditional rules applied by lawyers and the ordinary courts). There is no attempt to examine the many other types of compensation which may be payable under other types of rule or institution, e.g. sick pay, pensions, social security benefits, personal accident, life or sickness insurance, or criminal injuries compensation. Nor do I consider the question of legal compensation for sickness or congenital disability: there are in fact very few instances where legal rules imposing liability on other persons could lead to an award of damages in these cases.

The civil wrong of negligence

The main ground for the award of compensation for death or personal injury suffered in accidents is negligence. Although there are many technical aspects of the tort (civil wrong) of negligence, its basic structure is simple: a person (the plaintiff or claimant) who can prove that he suffered personal injury or other loss as the result of the fault or carelessness of another person (the defendant) may recover compensation ('damages') from the latter. The first requirement is that the defendant should owe 'a duty of care' to the plaintiff. This test enables judges to exclude certain persons from the benefit of the tort of negligence by saying that they were not, immediately prior to the accident, within the normal range of potential risk created by the defendant's activity. The usual test is whether an ordinary person in the defendant's position should have foreseen that a failure on his part to take care might endanger a person in the plaintiff's position. So, for instance, the manufacturer of an article owes a duty of care towards persons who ultimately use the article; the repairer of a motor-vehicle owes a duty of care to third persons, such as pedestrians, who use public roads and may be injured by a defective repair; but an occupier of land does not owe an ordinary duty of care (under the tort of negligence) towards a trespasser injured on his land.[1]

The second requirement for the tort of negligence is that the defendant's conduct should have fallen below the standard of care which would have been shown by the 'reasonable' or ordinary person in the same situation. Did the defendant do something which the ordinary person would not have done? or, did he fail to do something which the ordinary man would have done, in order to avoid the risk of an accident? The standard of reasonable care is a very flexible one which gives the judges a limited discretion to decide whether or not to impose liability in borderline cases. The judges balance the degree of risk of causing an accident against the cost and feasibility of taking action to avoid the risk: might the ordinary man have caused this accident in these circumstances, or would he have been able to avoid it?

The third requirement is that the negligent conduct of the defendant should be proved in fact to have *caused* the injury or loss which the plaintiff suffered, and that the loss or injury should not, in the eye of the law, be too unusual a consequence of that conduct. (Lawyers say it must not be 'too remote' a consequence.) The test of causation depends on a common-sense application of scientific, medical and mechanical knowledge. The test of remoteness is a judicial technique to protect the defendant from liability for unusual or abnormal consequences of his negligent conduct. Here again, the judges are exercising a measure of discretion between labelling usual or normal consequences as 'not too remote' (that is, consequences for which compensation will be awarded), and unusual or abnormal consequences as 'too

---

[1] A trespasser is a person who does not have permission to be on private land.

remote' (for which no compensation is given). The current test for deciding that a consequence is 'too remote' is whether it was reasonably foreseeable that the negligent conduct in question might cause loss or injury of the same category or type as that which in fact was caused.[1] The courts do not require foresight of the precise details of the accident,[2] but of the general type of causation involved (e.g. fire, explosion or collision) and the general category of consequence (e.g. personal injury, nervous shock, financial loss irrespective of physical loss, or damage to chattels). The question 'How likely must a risk be before it is reasonably foreseeable?' is answered by saying that it is a reasonably foreseeable risk if the reasonable or ordinary man would not only direct his mind to the particular risk but would also take measures to avoid the risk.[3] An important rule under the heading of remoteness of damage is that the defendant who is found to be liable in tort 'must take his victim as he finds him'. This means that the defendant will be liable for all the personal injuries suffered by the plaintiff, even where the plaintiff suffered more severely because of his previous medical or physical condition. So a successful plaintiff who is susceptible to injury on account of brittle bones or a thin skull will be compensated to the full extent of his injury, despite the fact that the normal or average person would not have suffered as severely.

The onus of proof in negligence cases

English law puts the onus of proving negligence on the plaintiff, who will therefore fail in his claim for compensation if he cannot prove the fault of the defendant. From the point of view of the accident victim, however, it is usually a matter of chance whether there were witnesses of the accident and of the events leading up to it. Together with a research assistant, Steven Hartz, I conducted a pilot survey in Oxford in 1967–68 to test techniques for a social survey of the operation of accident law.[4] All the 989 cases (remaining after a pre-test) of personal injury in traffic accidents in the Oxford City police district in 1965 were investi-

---

[1] *The Wagon Mound* [1961] Appeal Cases 388.
[2] *Hughes* v *Lord Advocate* [1963] Appeal Cases 837.
[3] *The Wagon Mound* (No. 2) [1967] 1 Appeal Cases 617.
[4] A short account of the survey is in 119 (1969) New Law Journal 492.

gated by a postal survey; there was a response rate of 74.2% and from the replies a selection was made of all those who were away from work (or unable to carry on their normal activities) for six weeks or more (a total of 90). A questionnaire of 110 questions was used in interviews with these ninety accident victims and a further questionnaire was sent to the lawyers who handled the successful claims for damages made by 45% of the 90.

The accident victims who failed to obtain any damages were asked for a statement of the reasons for their failure: half of these blamed their failure on lack of evidence—there were no independent witnesses of the accident, or the available evidence was insufficient or unreliable. From the point of view of accident victims as a whole, it cannot be said that the needs of the 45% who obtained no damages, nor the merits of their claims to be compensated, differ in any way from that of the group who succeeded in obtaining damages: the only difference is the extrinsic fact that the latter group were lucky enough to have found sufficient evidence to convince an insurance company (anticipating the decision of a court) that another person was at fault in causing the accident. Proof of the demerits of another person, not of the merits of the victim's claim, is the crucial point.

In a few situations, legislation has altered the onus of proof so that the accident victim's claim does not depend on the availability of evidence of fault. One situation concerns the liability of a public authority for personal injuries caused by a failure to repair a highway: the authority is liable unless it can prove that it took reasonable care to prevent danger to traffic.[1] There is another exception following a practical rule of evidence, known as *res ipsa loquitur*: if the situation in which the accident occurred was in the exclusive control of the defendant (or his employees), and the accident is one which would not normally have happened unless someone was at fault, the courts are prepared to infer that the defendant (or one of his employees) must have been at fault, unless he can explain how the accident happened and can show that he was not at fault. However, in many accident situations this rule does not assist a victim, e.g. in factories and on the roads it is seldom that only one person (or one enterprise) is in control of all the relevant aspects of the situation.

---

[1] Highways (Miscellaneous Provisions) Act 1961.

Other legal rules on liability

Many statutes, such as the factories legislation, set standards of safety and impose criminal penalties for violation of these standards. Often a person may have been injured as a consequence of an act done in breach of such a statutory duty, but the statute is normally silent on the question whether the injured person may sue for damages in a civil claim. In the absence of any express provision in the Act, the courts have pretended to decide the question on the basis of the presumed intention of Parliament: did Parliament intend a person who breaks the statutory standard to be liable to pay compensation to anyone injured, or did it intend the criminal penalty (usually a fine) to be the sole legal consequence of the breach? The answer to this question depends on judicial guesswork, which therefore really decides whether or not the accident victim receives damages. In the case of statutes and regulations controlling the use of roads and the safety of motor-vehicles, the courts have decided that it could not have been the intention of Parliament that a trivial breach of a statutory standard, for which a small fine would be appropriate, should lead to liability for an award of damages limited only by the actual extent of the claimant's loss or injury: the claimant must go further and prove the defendant's negligence. Although in these cases the defendant's breach of the statutory standard may be one factor assisting the plaintiff to prove negligence, it is not conclusive evidence of negligence. However, in the case of industrial accidents, the courts regularly permit an employee to recover damages from his employer, without proof of the employer's fault, if it is shown that the employer was in breach of a legislative rule about safety of the premises, machinery or equipment. But in practice, for a variety of reasons, injured employees do not enjoy a high success rate in claiming damages: no reliable statistics are available but recent estimates have been that only 10–20% succeed.

A defendant is occasionally liable, irrespective of his fault, for creating a risk in the course of which the plaintiff suffered personal injuries. Some of these instances are the result of law decided by the judges: thus, an occupier of land is liable when a dangerous accumulation on his land (e.g. a large quantity of gas, water, or electricity) escapes outside and causes damage (personal injuries are probably covered by this rule). Another judge-made doctrine provides the most important instance of liability without fault in English law: this is the doctrine of vicarious liability, under which an employer is responsible (jointly with his employee) to pay damages if his employee injures the plaintiff by a tort committed 'in the course of his employment'. A high proportion of tort claims are in practice brought against employers, since they are more likely to be insured, and, even if they are not insured, they are more likely to have assets to satisfy a judgment against them.[1] Liability without proof of fault is sometimes imposed by statutes. Thus, the person who keeps a wild animal is liable for damage (including personal injuries) caused by the animal; an airline is liable without fault for injuries to a passenger in an international flight; and the operator of a nuclear installation is liable for injury or damage caused by the escape of ionizing radiations.

The objectives of the law of torts on accidents

There is a variety of objectives suggested for tort law in this field.

(a) *The deterrence of careless or antisocial conduct.* This objective is achieved only in a haphazard way, however, since tort law comes into operation only when the proved carelessness of one person in fact causes loss or injury to another person. Tort law is potentially applicable to all carelessness, but it is applied only to those cases where the risk involved in carelessness actually results in injurious consequences. But the law of negligence could have some general deterrent effect, in that people realize that carelessness can, on occasion, involve them in unpleasant legal consequences. The institution of liability insurance and the doctrine of vicarious liability[2] have largely undermined the deterrence objective in the tort of negligence. If a potential defendant knows that he is covered by a liability insurance policy (whether taken out voluntarily or under compulsion of law—as in the case of motor insurance and employer's liability insurance) he

---

[1] In theory, an employer who pays damages under this doctrine may recover the amount from his employee, but this rule is not followed in practice: nearly all insurance companies have agreed not to take advantage of the rule if they are responsible for insuring the employer against his vicarious liability.

[2] See above.

knows that he is not carrying on his activity under the risk of a catastrophic penalty if he causes a serious loss through his carelessness. A man's fear of an increased premium when he renews his insurance after claims against him have been met by his insurance company has only a limited deterrent effect, and is very different from the original deterrent purpose of the tort of negligence—that the wrongdoer himself should pay. A further difficulty in accepting the deterrence objective is that the tortious penalty for carelessness bears no necessary relation to the degree of blameworthiness, since the amount of damages depends on the seriousness of the harm actually caused by the carelessness: a trivial lack of care may cause an extensive amount of damage, whereas a flagrant act of recklessness may cause little damage, or even none at all. Deterrence, it is submitted, is better achieved by the criminal law, by a man's fear for his own personal safety, and by a social conscience educated by publicity on accident prevention.

Furthermore, the concept of legal fault is a purely objective one based on average standards in the community, and it does not correspond to personal fault or moral blameworthiness in the individual defendant[1]; the mental and physical capabilities of the individual man are ignored by the law. Many accidents are caused by factors such as lack of experience, errors of judgment, unknown physical or visual defects, below-average speeds of perception or reaction, or psychological tensions. We do not ignore these factors when assessing moral blame, but the law ignores them in attributing responsibility to pay for accidents. Nor can we deter individuals from causing accidents by imposing on them standards which they personally are unable to achieve.

(*b*) *Compensation*. The major objective of the modern civil law on accidents is to compensate injured persons for their loss and injury.[2] The same objective underlies the statutory compulsion upon motorists and employers to insure against the risk of tortious liability: this compulsion is the result of the legislators' wish to provide funds for successful plaintiffs—not their wish to protect potential defendants against bankruptcy or a crippling

---

[1] Nor is there personal fault in an employer who is held vicariously liable for the negligence of his employee: see above p. 35.

[2] This is also the objective of the Criminal Injuries Compensation scheme which is financed directly by the taxpayer.

financial liability. But the common law is an individualistic system, in that it thinks of one individual, the plaintiff, seeking money from another individual, the defendant; the law conceives of the defendant paying out of his own pocket, and therefore requires a sound reason for compelling him to pay for another man's loss. Hence, the traditional common law approach requires that several reasons should coincide before an injured person is entitled to an award of damages: (i) The plaintiff's needs—he has suffered some injury or loss; and (ii) The plaintiff's merits—he was not to blame for the accident[1]; and (iii) The demerits of the defendant—there is a justification for making the defendant pay compensation for that injury or loss, *viz.* the defendant not only caused the loss or injury, but was at fault in so causing it. In the eye of the common law, the plaintiff's needs and his blamelessness are not sufficient grounds for entitlement to compensation: in addition, there must be a separate ground to justify shifting the loss on to the shoulders of the defendant. Thus, the legal rules discriminate between accident victims, not on the issue of their relative needs for compensation, but on the issue whether the human shortcomings of another person formed part of the causation of the accident. From the point of view of the accident victims, the decision on the latter issue is often a pure chance. The law still continues with this philosophy despite the fact that, since liability insurance is now widespread (and compulsory in some areas), the defendant hardly ever pays out of his own pocket. If we looked at the substance of the matter today, we might ask why proof of another man's fault is the only ground for permitting an injured man to have access to insurance funds for his compensation. After all, the law merely says that a man is 'liable', and is not concerned whether he can actually find the money to pay the damages: it is insurance which in practice provides the money. But the legal rules of liability have not been modified to take account of the ways in which insurance funds are collected, and by which risks can be spread over a large group in society.[2] The law has adjusted neither its objectives, nor its rules, to take account of the situation in the twentieth century: it still clings to the nineteenth century approach, which is con-

---

[1] This rule has now been modified by legislation: see pp. 51–52.
[2] To a limited extent the doctrine of vicarious liability (see p. 35) does have the effect of spreading risks.

trary to the philosophy supporting the modern Welfare State, the Criminal Injuries Compensation scheme, or the institution of sick pay and other privately-organized group schemes of support.

There are almost no statistics available to show what proportion of persons injured in accidents receive any damages under the legal system of providing compensation. In the Oxford survey,[1] only 45.5% of the ninety injured persons who were off work, or unable to carry on their normal lives, for six weeks or more, obtained any damages; about 25% of these suffered a reduction on account of contributory negligence,[2] which means that only one-third of the total were receiving (in theory at least) full common law damages. Of the 45.5% who obtained some damages, about one-fifth recovered less than their actual financial loss (*viz*. loss of past or future earnings, and out-of-pocket expenses— excluding anything for pain and suffering, disfigurement, loss of use of a limb, etc.).[3] It is hard to accept that these figures indicate that the tort system is functioning satisfactorily, and that the law compensates all those who deserve, from a social point of view, to be compensated.

In the writer's opinion, it is only the existence of non-legal sources of compensation which prevent the public from seeing the glaring anomalies of the legal system of damages. In the Oxford survey, for instance, 71% of the ninety injured persons received some social security benefits (including 6% receiving industrial injuries benefit, and 7% national assistance (now replaced by supplementary benefits)); 42% of the ninety received some sick pay from employers (77% of the ninety were employed); and 73% of the ninety received financial support during their disability from other members of their families. From these sources, some financial assistance is quickly provided for accident victims, so that none are left destitute.

(*c*) *Protecting freedom of action.* The objective here is to avoid discouraging socially useful activities. The dominance of neglig- ence as the legal ground for awarding compensation is the result

---

[1] See above pp. 32–33.

[2] See below pp. 51–53.

[3] See below pp. 45–46. When the same analysis is made of all the ninety victims, the result is that from all sources of compensation (including social security benefits) 12% of the ninety received less than 20% of their financial losses and 64% less than their actual financial losses.

of nineteenth-century developments: before then, the law found little difficulty in holding a man strictly liable to compensate another injured by his actions, whether or not those actions were careless or anti-social in some other way. The concept of individualism, and the acceptance of *laissez faire*, provided the background to the nineteenth-century developments. To hold a man liable only if he is negligent gives wide protection to his freedom of action—it encourages him to pursue all lawful forms of activity, secure in the knowledge that he will not have to bear the burden of compensating those who are injured by his actions despite his taking ordinary care. If the nineteenth-century judges thought that society expected them to give protection to the bodily security and well-being of the individual, it would have been best achieved by strict liability (irrespective of fault) upon the person whose action caused bodily injury. Strict liability would not only give the potential victim some assurance of compensation, but it might have encouraged people to take all possible care, in the knowledge that if their actions did cause injury they would have to pay for the cost. (In the modern world, of course, strict liability results in potential defendants taking out liability insurance.) However, the decision of the judges last century to make compensation normally depend on proof of the actor's fault reflected a value-judgment that it was more important for society to avoid discouraging initiative and enterprise than to assure citizens that if they were injured they would be compensated. It was assumed in that century that these objectives were inconsistent—that the law could not, at one and the same time, both encourage initiative and useful activities and also assure the potential victim of accidents that he would be compensated. The institution of insurance, and the concept of the welfare state, has made possible the separation of these objectives: if potential defendants are insured against any legal liability towards others, they are not inhibited from pursuing any lawful activity by the fear of crippling financial losses if others are injured in the course of the activity. Except for the cost of the insurance premium, which is a definite, known, sum and can therefore be budgetted for in the current year's expenses, there need be no financial inhibition against engaging in activities involving risk to others.

The tort of negligence puts the risk of all but negligently-caused accidents upon the potential victims of a man's activities;

a man acts at his own risk in so far as he is proved to have been careless, but at the risk of others in all other respects. It is difficult today to accept this approach, particularly when a man may increase the risk of injury to others by his decision to engage in a particular activity, e.g. his decision not to walk but to use a motor-vehicle for his transport clearly increases the risks of injury to others.

(*d*) *Vindictiveness or revenge.* This was an aim of early tort law, but few people are nowadays likely to support this objective. Some appeasement of the injured person, however, is still a factor to be considered: many ordinary people think that a careless wrong-doer ought to be made to pay (and to be seen to be made to pay), even if he is not made to suffer a criminal penalty. The fact that insurance almost invariably pays the damages does not altogether remove the layman's vague feeling that since the payment is made in the name of the defendant, he is somehow involved, and that the concept of fairness and justice is being met.

(*e*) *Accident prevention: the need for an inquest.* There is always a desire for a public inquest when a serious accident has occurred. To a certain extent, the law of torts may satisfy the feeling that when something has gone seriously wrong, and loss or injury has resulted, there should be an inquiry or inquest to see whether it could have been avoided, and, if so, who was to blame. Although only a minute fraction (perhaps only about 1%) of all accident cases actually reach the court-room, the injured person may feel satisfaction in knowing that there is always the chance that his case might lead to a hearing in public. Similarly, the fact that lawyers or insurance officials are investigating the accident may make him feel that his case is being taken seriously, and that 'something is being done' to attribute responsibility for the accident and perhaps to prevent similar accidents in future. Sometimes an inquiry into the possibility of fault or tortious responsibility may assist in the aim of accident prevention: it may lead to the discovery of better methods of preventing similar accidents, and it may fix better standards of care in the type of activity in question. The problem about achieving this objective of the tort rules is that it is often in the very cases where the need for a public inquest is greatest that none is held, because in a clear case of negligence the defendant's insurance company accepts liability without a fight. In any case, the small fraction of

accident cases actually heard by the courts are selected by those
defendants or their insurers who choose to fight, not by a public
agency which thinks that these are the cases which should be
investigated in the interests of accident prevention. Even where
there is a court hearing of an accident case, there is little chance
of publicity for the outcome, either in national or local news-
papers. If the defendant is defended by a professional or trade
body (such as the Medical Defence Union) there is sometimes a
mention of the case in a subsequent issue of the journal of that
body, so that other members should know what standards of
care have been accepted as reasonable by the court. But neither
the court nor the plaintiff can require that publicity should be
given to the decision, nor is there any public authority to give it
publicity in the interests of accident prevention. The lack of
publicity, and the random selection of the cases which are actually
heard by the courts, undermines the achievement of any objective
of accident prevention by the law of negligence.

Assessment of damages for personal injuries

There is no coherent principle to explain the various rules which
govern the assessment of damages for death or personal injuries.
The basic principle is said to be full compensation in each individual case *viz*. that the victim of the accident should be placed
in the same financial position as he would be in if he had not been
injured. No ceilings are fixed for the amounts which may be
awarded as damages, but there are many rules and practices
followed by the judges which have the effect of restricting the
principle of full compensation. Claims for damages for personal
injuries are always decided by judges sitting alone, without juries;
the Court of Appeal, in order to achieve some uniformity of
awards of damages for personal injuries, has ruled that a judge
sitting alone should decide these cases, unless there are exceptional circumstances.[1] However, it is only in a minute fraction
of the total number of accident cases that the judges themselves
apply the rules on assessment of damages. The vast majority of
claims are settled by negotiation without the need for a judicial
decision, with the result that the rules are in practice applied by
solicitors, insurance assessors, trade union representatives, etc.;

---

[1] *Ward* v. *James* [1966] 1 Queen's Bench 273.

the judges remain in the background as the ultimate arbiters if a settlement cannot be reached between the parties. Items of loss which can be calculated exactly up to the time of the trial or settlement, such as loss of earnings and expenses[1] already incurred, are given in full as 'special damages': in this respect the courts do give a total indemnity. All other types of loss are dealt with by the award of a single lump sum[2] as 'general damages', to cover all the estimates which the judges make about losses which cannot be exactly calculated.[3]

(*a*) *Future loss of earnings.* An important aspect of general damages is the plaintiff's expected future loss of earnings (subject to a discount because he will receive the money as a lump sum earlier than he could have earned it).[4] The period for which his future loss of earnings is calculated is not his pre-accident expectation of life, but his post-accident expectation. If, as a result of the accident, the plaintiff is expected to live for a shorter period of years, his damages for loss of earnings will be limited to his shortened life. All that is awarded for the 'lost years' is the nominal sum of money given for loss of expectation of life.[5] This shows the assumption made by the judges that in the case of a living plaintiff he is the only one to be compensated: no account is taken of the fact that many injured persons are and will be supporting a wife and family, whose expectation of life will not have been shortened by the accident, but who will be adversely affected by the loss of earnings during the 'lost years'.[6] When the plaintiff survives the accident, the judges do not think in terms of compensating the family unit as a whole, but this is the approach when a father or husband has been killed in an accident. In a 'fatal accident' claim,[7] compensation is assessed on the basis of the number of years during which the widow and

---

[1] No claim may be made for expenses of hospital and medical treatment if the injured person in fact received the treatment free of cost under the National Health Service.

[2] See below pp. 48–49, on the question of lump sums.

[3] See below p. 50, on the itemization of heads of damages.

[4] No account is taken of how the plaintiff would normally have spent his money.

[5] *Oliver* v. *Ashman* [1962] 2 Queen's Bench 210: see below pp. 45–46.

[6] For a recent illustration of the injustice of this rule, see *McCann* v. *Sheppard* [1973] 1 Weekly Law Reports 540.

[7] See below pp. 54–55.

children expected to be financially dependent on the earnings of the deceased, and this in turn depends on the number of future 'earning' years which the deceased could have expected just before the accident. Hence, in a fatal accident claim, the family is compensated for their loss of financial support during the 'lost' years. If a husband or father is seriously injured in an accident and his expectation of life is shortened, the amount of compensation available to support his family after his death depends on the fortuitous timing of the settlement of his claim. If his claim is settled while he still survives, this will adversely affect the future financial prospects of his family, who would be better compensated if they could claim after his death. There are fixed periods after the accident within which claims for damages must be commenced by legal action (three years in the case of personal injuries) and a legal adviser cannot risk too much delay. The result is an anomaly in that the assessment of damages may be affected by the period of time a seriously injured person holds on to life after the accident. The Law Commission has criticized[1] this rule and recommended[2] that compensation for the loss of earnings in the lost years should be based on the expected amount of these earnings, less the sum which the plaintiff would have spent on his own maintenance.[3]

In assessing damages for loss of future earnings, the judges make a deduction for 'contingencies of life'; these are the chances that, apart from the accident, the plaintiff might have become ill or been unemployed for various periods of his life, or even have died prematurely or been killed in another accident. No account is taken of the risk of future inflation in the value of money,[4] and little account is taken of the expectation that the levels of wages and salaries will rise in the future. The courts seem to assume that prudent investment of the damages will cope with

---

[1] Report on Personal Injury Litigation—Assessment of Damages (Law Com. No. 56) (July 1973), paras. 55–91.

[2] *Ibid.*, para. 87

[3] This is the rule in Australia: *Skelton* v. *Collins* (1966) 39 Australian Law Journal Reports 480.

[4] *Mitchell* v. *Mulholland* (No. 2) [1972] 1 Queen's Bench 65. (Evidence of an economist as to rate of future inflation was treated by the court as inadmissible. But compare the obligation of the government to hold an annual review of the rates of social security benefits: section 39 of the Social Security Act 1973.)

inflation, and the Law Commission considers that the 'primary' way of tackling the question of inflation is to assess damages on the basis that the plaintiff will be able to invest his damages at the rate receivable at the date of the award in good growth equities.[1] But it is doubtful whether the ordinary man has ready access to sound investment advice, and, even if he did, whether equity investment can be relied on to keep pace with inflation.

(b) The 'multiplier' system. This is the method by which judges calculate the present value of the capital sum needed to compensate the plaintiff for an annual loss (e.g. of earnings) spread over a future period. The capital sum cannot be the full amount of the estimated annual loss multiplied by the full number of years of the future period (e.g. the number of years from the date of the judgment till the plaintiff's normal retiring age) since this would ignore the interest or dividends which the investment of the capital sum could earn over that period. In the multiplier system the judge first assesses the annual sum of the plaintiff's loss, and then chooses a number of years' 'purchase' by which to multiply the annual loss (e.g. 12 years). In the House of Lords this system has recently been approved as the normal and best method, on the ground that it is based on the experience of judges and practitioners:[2] as Lord Reid put it, 'Judges and counsel have a wealth of experience which is an adequate guide to the selection of the multiplier and any expert evidence is rightly discouraged'.[3] The 'expert evidence' in question would be actuarial figures for the sum needed, based on the plaintiff's expectation of life, and his other circumstances, to buy an annuity to cover his annual loss. The Law Commission has criticized the multiplier system and has recommended that the courts should accept actuarial evidence in the assessment of damages, and that there should be some actuarial

---

[1] Report on Personal Injury Litigation (see Note 1, p. 43) para. 227 (as suggested by Lord Diplock in *Mallett* v. *McMonagle* [1970] Appeal Cases 166, 175–76). This approach implies that the damages should be computed on an actuarial basis, rather than on the traditional 'multiplier' method (on which see above). In para. 229 of their Report, the Law Commission say that a set of official actuarial tables might include a factor to take some account of future inflation.

[2] *Taylor* v. *O'Connor* [1971] Appeal Cases 115.

[3] *Ibid.*, at p. 128. (It is submitted that this reason is inadequate: witch-doctors also have a 'wealth of experience' in practice.)

tables published on an official basis, so that their accuracy and authority would be accepted by the courts.[1]

Categories of non-economic losses

(a) *Pain and suffering.* In a personal injury claim, damages may be awarded both for pain and suffering up to the date of the trial (or settlement out of court) and also for the pain and suffering which the injured person is likely to suffer in the future. This general heading may also cover other mental aspects of the plaintiff's suffering, such as his neurosis caused by the injury, or his knowledge that his life has been shortened, that he is disabled or disfigured,[2] or that his disability will limit his enjoyment of life. But a victim rendered permanently unconscious cannot receive damages for pain or suffering he does not experience.[3]

(b) *Loss of expectation of life.* This head of damages compensates for the shortening of the victim's life; it is assessed on the basis of loss of 'prospective happiness', and a low, traditional, sum of about £500 is given.[4] (The sum is likely to be awarded under this heading whether the injured person is an adult or a child,[5] and whether the award is made to a surviving plaintiff or to the estate of a victim who was killed.[6])

(c) *Loss of amenities.* This heading compensates the injured person for loss of the capacity to enjoy life, as distinct from the length of life; it includes impairment of the plaintiff's health or energy, inability to have children, and loss of marriage prospects. It does not depend on the plaintiff's own realization of his loss.[7] It

---

[1] Report on Personal Injury Litigation (see Note 1, p. 43) paras. 215–30.

[2] Damages may also take account of the plaintiff's embarrassment resulting from the disfigurement, or of a woman's reduced prospects of marriage because of disfigurement.

[3] *Wise* v. *Kaye* [1962] 1 Queen's Bench 638.

[4] *Benham* v. *Gambling* [1941] Appeal Cases 157; *Yorkshire Electricity Board* v. *Naylor* [1968] Appeal Cases 529 (£500 for normal adult).

[5] *Cain* v. *Wilcock* [1968] 1 Weekly Law Reports 1961 (£500 for child of 2½ years).

[6] See below pp. 54–55.

[7] *West and Son Ltd.* v. *Shephard* [1964] Appeal Cases 326. The problem of an unconscious, or nearly-unconscious plaintiff, who is unlikely to gain any greater consciousness of his condition, is a special one, which has divided the courts and the commentators: see the Australian case of *Skelton* v. *Collins* (1966) 39 Australian Law Journal Reports 480, and the Law Commission's Working Paper No. 41 (1971) paras. 81–89.

includes disfigurement, and anything which interferes with a normal life; for instance, if the injured person can no longer play a sport or follow a leisure interest. This heading is quite separate from loss of earnings; often a loss of amenity may not reduce the victim's ability to earn an income, as would be the case in a lawyer's loss of the hand with which he does not write. Damages will be increased if the plaintiff has a definite loss under this heading, e.g. if the lawyer's recreation before losing his hand was piano-playing. The law treats life as worth living in all its aspects, and thus its impairment is worth compensating, irrespective of the question whether one has a happy life or not: a person may have just as happy a life after the accident as before, despite his inability to continue some activities in which he previously took part.

Method of assessing damages for non-economic losses

(*a*) *Medical evidence*. In assessing pain and suffering and loss of expectation of life or of amenities, the courts are naturally very dependent on medical opinions. Frequently the parties exchange written reports by their medical experts, but it is possible that in the case of serious injuries the medical advisers will be called upon to give oral evidence to the court to supplement their reports. But the courts often ask the medical expert to deal with a prognosis which is beset with uncertainties: there is the uncertainty whether the condition of the patient may worsen in the future (e.g. that a head injury may lead to epilepsy) and even when it is virtually certain that a particular condition may develop in the future (e.g. osteo-arthritis in a joint) there is uncertainty as to the timing and the seriousness of the condition. Medical men are compelled by the legal system to deal in guesswork, because the law insists on quantifying the compensation once and for all, and in advance of developments. The trouble is that lawyers try to reduce all these medical uncertainties to a precise calculation of a single sum of money because the rule is that only one action for damages can be brought: if the plaintiff's injuries later turn out to be more serious than his medical advisers expected at the time of the trial (or when he settled his claim), he cannot re-open his claim in order to recover more compensation.

(*b*) *The unofficial scale of awards*. Lawyers face difficult problems in assessing damages for items where only an estimate is possible.

The courts have developed over the years a conventional range of awards[1] to cover their guesswork in putting a monetary value on items such as pain and suffering, and loss of a limb: the awards are 'fair' in the sense that they are in conformity with other awards in similar cases, but the judges make no attempt to see that their awards are adequate in fact. There is an efficient system of monthly reports[2] of the amounts of damages in any cases of personal injuries which will be a useful guide to future awards: the result is an unofficial scale of awards for common injuries, upon which lawyers base their arguments. But the judge makes a special award for each individual case, so that he has some discretion in fixing the amount. (The individualization of the award is, of course, a major reason for the great delay in the settlement of claims, and for the considerable expense involved in handling claims for damages.[3]) Lawyers may sometimes persuade the court that the scale for a particular injury should be increased on account of inflation or other changed circumstances,[4] but the system of an unofficial scale has many disadvantages. The Law Commission considered whether it should recommend a legislative tariff of awards for non-pecuniary loss, tied to a cost of living index,[5] but it concluded that there was not, among those who were consulted, 'any real enthusiasm for this innovation'.[6]

---

[1] See Kemp and Kemp on the *Quantum of Damages* (3rd ed., 1967).

[2] *Current Law*, a monthly publication designed to incorporate all legal changes and decisions, gives these reports under the heading 'Damages'.

[3] Accurate figures for the United Kingdom are not available to show the cost of administering the present system of damages for death or personal injuries caused by negligence. In the United States of America, a *Federal Study on Automobile Insurance and Compensation* found that a little over 50% of the total insurance premiums paid by motorists in respect of their tort liability was used in paying for the expense of administering the system (insurance companies' overheads and expenses, including commissions, legal fees of both claimants and insurance companies, etc.) so that accident victims were receiving less than 50% of the money paid out by motorists. (*Motor Vehicle Crash Losses and their Compensation in the United States—A Report to Congress by the Department of Transportation* (1971) pp. 47–52.) Estimates of the corresponding figures in the United Kingdom have also put expenses at nearly 50% of the premiums paid. (Atiyah, *Accidents, Compensation and the Law* (1970) pp. 492–95).

[4] e.g. *Gardner* v. *Dyson* [1967] 1 Weekly Law Reports 1497 (increasing the scale figure for loss of an eye).

[5] Working Paper No. 41, paras. 95–104.

[6] Report on Personal Injury Litigation (see Note 1, p. 43) para. 35.

Since it is impossible to quantify in monetary terms the value of a lost limb, or the 'loss' involved in pain and suffering, the question should be asked why the attempt need be made. Damages are awarded because, as a matter of history, money was the only remedy the courts had available when claims in tort were first made. Perhaps the injured person can assuage his pain, or his loss of a limb, by buying something he could not have afforded before his accident; perhaps he can buy a better house, take up a new leisure activity, or enjoy more expensive holidays, to help him to forget the accident and its aftermath; perhaps he can use money to find alternative amenities to those of which he has been deprived. The courts have said that they are not using any concept of the 'price' of the injury *viz.* the price which a man would pay to avoid the injury, or the price an injured man would pay to get rid of the injury. There is no concept of a market, with its supply and demand, to fix a general value, and it must be accepted that the sums awarded by the courts are arbitrary, despite the fact that they are conventional and relatively uniform as between persons with similar injuries. But is money the only way to compensate a person for these non-economic losses? If there were available to disabled people a wide choice of recreational and other facilities to make up for their difficulties and their lost enjoyment of life, they might have a choice of substitute enjoyments, and there would then be sense in giving them money to use on whichever they fancy. But an award of damages does not of itself provide these facilities for a disabled person, who, on his own, can seldom commission the provision of a special facility just for himself. Handicapped people are usually dependent on governmental or community projects to provide them with specially-adapted housing or transport, parking and recreational facilities, access to buildings open to the public such as museums, theatres, cinemas, etc. The common law notion of giving the individual his own sum of money to find his own facilities on an individual basis is not realistic in the modern world, where the research and development costs of new aids for the disabled cannot be found by private enterprise. The conclusion must be that the lawyers' concept of non-economic losses, although well-intentioned, is often not a successful one.

(c) *The use of lump sums.* Damages for personal injuries are awarded as a single, lump sum, because the judges are not empowered to order the payment of a regular, periodic, amount as damages. The successful plaintiff can replace his loss of a regular income by using the lump sum to purchase an annuity, or by investing the sum himself. But the lump sum approach means that all future contingencies have to be assessed at a given point of time—when the court gives its decision or when the parties agree upon the settlement. We have already noted that the lump sum approach cannot cope directly with inflation in the future. More serious, however, is the objection that the once-and-for-all approach in assessing a lump sum to compensate the plaintiff for all the injurious consequences of his injury which may follow in an unforeseeable future cannot avoid unfairness to one side or the other. Suppose a case where there is a 10% chance of a serious medical complication occurring in the future: if the judge notionally assesses the damages on the basis that the complication ensues, and then reduces that sum by 90%, he will be able to award a definite sum now. But if the plaintiff does in fact later suffer the complication, he is seriously under-compensated, whereas if he escapes it, he is partly over-compensated. (The courts do not appear to have considered the insurance approach to this problem—what premium might be needed to insure the plaintiff in respect of the full notional sum against that contingency happening in the future; but the type of risk is not one which the regular insurance companies are normally willing to accept.) The once-and-for-all approach is also unfair in its estimates of the period of a person's future working life, or his chance of future redundancy or unemployment for other reasons. If the judge takes account of these factors by reducing his award, it is extremely unlikely that he will have hit upon the right discount to suit the plaintiff's future. The award will turn out in the actual circumstances to be either inadequate or over-generous in relation to other injured persons. Where the uncertainty is one of degree, e.g. how much sight or hearing the plaintiff will retain in five years' time, it is a remote chance that the judge will hit upon the figure he would have awarded had he known the future events. The assessment in advance cannot be attempted scientifically.

The judges have never explained why, in dealing with future contingencies, they have ignored the insurance principle, as exemplified in life and personal accident insurance, or in pension and social security schemes. The anomalies of the legal approach are partly avoided by the social security system which, by spreading a net of supplementary and other benefits ,under everyone, catches those who are afflicted by a worsening of their condition which was not anticipated, or properly provided for, at the time the lump sum was fixed. Much of the guesswork involved could be avoided by periodic payments in the form of a pension which could be varied (at least upwards) when an unforeseen contingency occurred. This system is used in Germany, and is being tried in Western Australia, but there are many difficulties in devising a suitable system for common law damages, as the Law Commission has found.[1] The Commission has recommended the use of a provisional award of a lump sum by the courts in some circumstances (e.g. where the medical prognosis is uncertain) with power to the plaintiff to apply for an increased sum.[2] But the legal system, as operated by lawyers and insurance companies, is out of step with the concept of periodical payments found in pension and sick pay schemes, social security benefits and the type of policies offered by private insurance companies for permanent sickness or disability.[3]

(d) *Itemization of heads of damages.* Until 1970, the judges usually refused to itemize the award of damages under the different headings: they merely said that they had taken them all into account in deciding what was the appropriate lump sum to award. This practice made it difficult to argue an appeal on the basis that the judge was wrong in his approach to the assessment of the plaintiff's loss under any one heading. The courts now[4] award interest at different rates on certain heads of damages, and for this purpose the court must itemize its award at least into three: (1) special damage (expenses and loss of earnings up to date); (2) non-pecuniary loss (e.g. pain and suffering); and (3) future

---

[1] Working Paper No. 41, paras. 222–52. In their final Report on Personal Injury Litigation (see Note 1, p. 43 above) paras. 26–30, the Commission decided that in the present system of compensation based on fault, 'it would not be worthwhile introducing period payments' (para. 29).

[2] Report (above) paras. 231–44. The Commission think that this power should be exercised only where the defendant is insured or a public authority (para. 240).

[3] Earnings-related periodic payments are the method of compensating for loss of earnings in the New Zealand statute introducing a comprehensive coverage for accidents, the Accident Compensation Act 1972.

[4] *Jefford* v. *Gee* [1970] 2 Queen's Bench 130.

expenses and future loss of earnings. (No interest is awarded on the third item.) But this still permits a judge to refuse to give the break-down of a number of his figures, so that his award may be difficult not only to understand but also to challenge. There is still too much of the 'High Priestly mystery' in this system, and the Law Commission has recommended[1] that legislation should compel the judges to itemize the heads of damages, e.g. the division between future loss of earnings and future expenses.

Items justifying a reduction in the assessment of damages

Once the defendant is held liable in tort for the plaintiff's personal injuries, the only grounds upon which the court may reduce the amount of damages are as follows:

(a) *Fault of the plaintiff.* If the plaintiff's loss or injury was caused partly by his own fault (contributory negligence), the court has a discretion to reduce the damages; the size of the reduction depends on the relative degree of the plaintiff's fault in comparison with the defendant's fault.[2] In the Oxford survey, one-quarter of those who obtained some tort damages received a sum which was reduced on this ground. The reduction is always assessed in terms of a percentage of the total amount which would have been awarded if the defendant had been solely to blame. This means that the amount of the reduction in money terms depends largely on the *extent* of the injuries or loss suffered by the plaintiff, and not simply on the relative seriousness of his fault. A plaintiff who is held only 10% at fault, but whose injuries merit an award of £20,000, will incur a much greater reduction in compensation than one who is held 80% at fault, but whose injuries are assessed at £1,000. This system may not be open to criticism where the defendant pays the damages himself, but it is a fortuitous 'penalty' when the damages are paid by an insurance company (and thus, ultimately, by the public or a wide section of the public), as is the position with accidents covered by compulsory insurance. In this situation it is the writer's opinion that the reduction should be assessed as a specific sum of money, like a fine, instead of a proportion of the actual loss; it would then depend on the various factors relevant to the assessment of a

---

[1] Report on Personal Injury Litigation (see Note 1, p. 43) above) paras. 181–214.
[2] Law Reform (Contributory Negligence) Act 1945.

criminal fine, including the financial position of the offender, his dependants, etc.

(b) *Taxation*. In assessing loss of earnings, past or future, a deduction is made for all taxes and social security contributions which would have been charged on the lost earnings, and only the net amount is given:[1] the result is that the defendant benefits from the imposition of taxation, and the Inland Revenue or Social Security Fund loses the corresponding amounts. This rule leads to a complicated tax inquiry in assessing damages and has been criticized, especially in respect of the court's having to guess the future levels of taxation.[2]

(c) *Social security benefits*. In general, an injured person is entitled to a social security benefit for the period of his disability, whether or not he is also entitled to claim damages for his injury. If he does recover damages from another person, or that person's insurance company, a partial deduction[3] in respect of his social security benefits will be made in assessing his loss of earnings: the amount of the deduction is one-half of the value of any industrial injury benefit, disablement benefit, sickness benefit or invalidity benefit which he has received, or probably will receive, for a period of five years from the accident.[4] By a judicial ruling, unemployment benefit is also deducted when assessing loss of earnings.[5] But charitable payments to the victim of a tort, made by the trustees of a charitable organization, are not deducted from damages.

---

[1] *British Transport Commission* v. *Gourley* [1956] Appeal Cases 185.

[2] Street, *Principles of the Law of Damages* (1962) at pp. 88–104. The Law Commission (Report on Personal Injury Litigation—see Note 1, p. 43) has recommended that no change should be made in this rule (paras. 49–52).

[3] The rule is a political compromise between opposing views: see the Report of the Departmental Committee on Alternative Remedies (Cmd. 6860) (1946). The Law Commission does not wish the compromise to be altered: Report (see Note 1, p. 43) paras. 132–137.

[4] Law Reform (Personal Injuries) Act 1948, Section 2(1). (Invalidity benefit was added to this list by the National Insurance Act 1971, section 3 and Schedule 5, para. 1.)

[5] *Foxley* v. *Olton* [1965] 2 Queen's Bench 306. Supplementary benefit received by the plaintiff was not taken into account. The Law Commission in its Report (see Note 1, p. 43) thinks that neither unemployment benefit nor supplementary benefit should be deducted from damages (para. 137).

(d) *Sick pay.* If an employer continues to pay wages to his employee who was injured in an accident, the employee's claim against a third person for damages is reduced by the amount of the sick pay. In a recent case,[1] the House of Lords has assumed that sick pay should be deducted from damages, whether the employer is bound to pay (by a statute, or under the contract of employment) or does so voluntarily, as a good employer interested in the welfare of his employees. (Until the result of any claim for damages is known, an employer can avoid this rule by making a series of loans to his employee, which are made on condition that they are to be repaid out of any damages which the employee subsequently receives.)

(e) *Pensions.* A disability pension paid to an injured employee under his employer's pension scheme is not deducted from any damages recoverable from a third person who is liable for the injury.[2] The courts have thus tried to draw a distinction between sick pay and a disability pension, but the distinction seems formalistic and narrow. It allows some injured persons to recover double compensation from public sources, *viz.* where both the damages and the disability pension are ultimately financed by the public via compulsory insurance, taxation, or (in the case of a local authority) by rates levied on property.

(f) *Private insurance.* If an injured person has taken out his own private accident or life insurance policy, and in fact he or his estate receives a payment under it from his insurance company, he (or his relatives after his death) can still claim full damages from another person who is legally liable for his injury or death.[3] The main reason for this rule is that the plaintiff had paid the insurance premium out of his own money, and that the 'independent relationship' (the contract) between the plaintiff and his own insurance company should not give an undeserved benefit to the defendant. This rule permits a person to wager or

---

[1] *Parry* v. *Cleaver* [1970] Appeal Cases 1 (criticised by Atiyah, 32 (1969) Modern Law Review 397).

[2] *Parry* v. *Cleaver, supra.*

[3] For accident insurance, see *Bradburn* v. *G.W. Railway* (1874) Law Reports 10 Exchequer 1, upheld recently in *Parry* v. *Cleaver, supra.* In the case of fatal accidents, the rule is laid down by statute: the Fatal Accidents Act 1959, Section 2(1).

'bet' on double recovery in respect of his death or personal injury.[1]

Claims following death

If a person is killed by the fault of another, the dependants[2] of the deceased have a claim (under the Fatal Accidents Acts 1846–1959) to recover a lump sum in respect of their loss of the pecuniary benefit which they would have received from the deceased but for his death.[3] (The relatives receive nothing for their grief or misery caused by the death;[4] nor does a child receive anything for the loss of parental care and affection.) The court assesses the total 'family' dependency on the deceased at the time of his death, and takes account of any future changes to be expected in this financial dependency. The same multiplier system[5] is used to turn the annual pecuniary loss of all the dependants into a single lump sum. By adjusting the number of years' purchase, the court attempts to make allowances for all future contingencies such as the possibility of the deceased's premature death or early retirement. Benefits received from the estate of the deceased are taken into account to reduce the damages, which are designed to compensate for loss of financial dependency. Where a widow and her dependent children claim, the bulk of the money awarded is given to the widow to control, since she is now

---

[1] Compare property insurance which is indemnity insurance, under which a person does not receive a fixed lump sum, but only the amount of the loss which he actually suffers. Under property insurance, the plaintiff is prevented from receiving double compensation: the insurance company, by the doctrine of subrogation, is entitled to stand in the place of the insured person and to bring a legal claim against the person who is legally liable for causing the loss or damage to the property.

[2] Wife, husband, parent, grand-parent, step-parent, child, grand-child, step-child, brother, sister, uncle, aunt (or the issue of any of the last four).

[3] See above (p. 43) for a short discussion of the way in which the court takes account of the deceased's expectation of life as it was *before* the accident.

[4] A conventional figure of £500 may be awarded for the benefit of the deceased's estate in respect of the deceased's loss of expectation of life. (See above p. 45.) The Law Commission proposes that this claim should be replaced by a new claim for 'bereavement' under which the surviving spouse, or the parents of an unmarried minor child who is killed by another's wrong, would receive a fixed sum of £1,000 (Report on Personal Injury Litigation (see Note 1, p. 43) paras. 177–180.

[5] See above p. 44.

the person responsible for providing for the children. By a 1971 statute,[1] the courts have been told, in assessing damages, to ignore the prospect of a widow remarrying (and even the fact that she has actually done so): this has the absurd result that a childless, young, widow who has excellent prospects of remarriage or of earning her own livelihood, may receive a larger award than a middle-aged widow whose marriage prospects are almost nil, but who has children to support.

Conclusion

The legal system of compensating accident victims by an award of damages obviously has many advantages for those who are fortunate enough to be successful in satisfying the legal tests: the aim is full compensation for each individual, and no ceilings are fixed upon the amounts recoverable; the award of damages is tailor-made to suit the needs of the individual; and many aspects of non-economic loss are covered. But its disadvantages outweigh these advantages: the system gives its benefits only to a proportion of all accident victims; it is very expensive to operate; it often involves considerable delay in any money reaching the accident victim whose needs are immediate; the lump sum approach requires prophetic insight into future contingencies; the system gives insufficient attention to needs of the family group as a whole; it makes the unrealistic assumption that a lump sum of money can meet all the needs of injured and disabled people; and it permits a number of victims to enjoy a considerable 'doubling up' of compensation for the same accident received from different sources. The Royal Commission on Civil Liability and Compensation for Personal Injury set up at the end of 1972 should be able to devise a much better system of compensation.[2]

---

[1] The Law Reform (Miscellaneous Provisions) Act 1971, section 4.

[2] On 1st April 1974, New Zealand introduced a comprehensive insurance scheme to cover all victims of all accidents no matter where or when the accidents occur, and irrespective of their causes: the Accident Compensation Act 1972 (as amended in 1973). In the United States of America and Canada, various 'no-fault' insurance schemes have recently come into effect to produce limited benefits for all victims of road accidents.

3 Damages for Personal Injury —Some Economic Issues[1]

N. A. DOHERTY and D. S. LEES

Introduction

In Section I we develop some economic issues which arise out of the 'fault' system of allocating accident costs. In Section II we present a numerical picture of the tort system of damages against a background of other institutions which allocate accident costs, and in Section III we compare fault with some alternative liability rules on the basis of economic criteria.

I

The tort system of damages does three things which arouse the interests of economists. In the first place tort imposes a set of financial penalties which may influence the number and severity of accidental injuries and the question arises as to whether the incentives embodied in common law contribute more to economic welfare than any alternative way of regulating accidents. Economists look at this problem in terms of a model of resource allocation in which the costs and benefits to society from alternative use of available resources are compared. If an economic system is such that it is possible, by reallocating resources, to increase the welfare

[1] The parts of the original conference paper on which this chapter is based, dealing with a general review of compensation arrangements, have since been published by the authors in *Lloyds Bank Review*, April 1973. We concentrate here on the 'fault' system but this should be seen against the more general background. The research on which the chapter is based is supported by a grant from the Social Science Research Council, for which grateful acknowledgment is made.

of some without reducing the welfare of others, then the system is said to be 'inefficient'.

Secondly, the tort system redistributes income and wealth. Ostensibly the loss is shifted from the injured person to another who has been shown to be negligent, though in fact the redistribution is normally from those who pay liability insurance premiums. Since those who cause accidents are themselves often exposed to the risk of injury (e.g. motorists) then the process may also be seen as one in which the income of the individual is redistributed from times of health to times of impairment. In the absence of a dictatorial regime, these redistributions can only be evaluated by reference to individual and social preferences, and, although it may not be possible to identify these preferences, it may be possible to say whether a particular system is sensitive to them.

Thirdly, the tort system not only reallocates resources, it also consumes them. Transaction costs are incurred at various stages. The bulk of these costs are incurred in underwriting a system of liability insurance, though these are added to by the cost of disputing liability and negotiating settlement for particular cases. These costs provide a measure of the price to society of justice or whatever is achieved by the tort system. Further discussion of transaction costs is left to Section II and the remainder of this section is devoted to discussion of the regulatory and compensatory functions.

Personal injuries are typically associated with different activities which may be more or less dangerous. These may range from running a home to operating a coal mine; from watching the television to flying an aeroplane. If someone engages in one of these activities, it is presumably because the benefits to him outweigh the costs even though those costs may include a risk of injury or death. Difficulties arise if the costs and benefits of the activity are not confined to the individual who decides on how and how much of the activity should be undertaken. Thus it is possible that, whilst one level of an activity is beneficial to the individual, another level is best for society as a whole. There is a divergence between private and social cost.

The problem can be resolved by imposing an outright prohibition or by bestowing unrestrained liberty on activities depending upon which approach gives the higher net benefits. Another approach would be to reallocate the cost of accidents.

The problem with the 'all or nothing' approach is that it precludes intermediate solutions that may be desirable. For example, a situation in which driving is unrestricted may be preferable to outright prohibition. However, it may be possible to increase welfare further by inducing a small reduction (or increase) in total man hours driven. The fine tuning may be provided by negotiation between the parties involved [4:5]. Furthermore, if negotiation between the parties is costless, then from the viewpoint of economic efficiency, the optimal level of accidents is independent of the allocation of costs. This can best be illustrated by an example. The 'optimal' level of accidents for an activity occurs when there are no further opportunities for increasing net social benefits (benefits minus costs) by either changing the level of the activity or by investing in safety devices. Using the example of collisions between motorists and pedestrians, that level would prevail if motorists were liable for accident costs, or if pedestrians were liable. If there were potential social benefits from changes in the activity level or incorporation of safety devices, it would pay the person to whom the benefits accrue either to change the activity level etc. or to 'bribe'[1] the other party to do so. However, in the real world where there are transaction costs it becomes important from an economic efficiency viewpoint to allocate liability to that party who can most efficiently approach the optimum level of safety [3]. Staying with the example of motorists and pedestrians, the relevant issue is whether accidents can be reduced more cheaply by allocating liability to *motorists*, who are then provided with an incentive to drive more slowly and carefully, to campaign for pedestrians to wear white coats and for local authorities to construct safer pedestrian precincts; to *pedestrians*, who will not have to campaign to be induced to wear white coats, but may collectively bribe motorists to drive more carefully; or even to *local authorities*, who may then wish to plan roadways and pedestrian precincts in such a way as to limit the exposure of pedestrians to motor cars—or vice versa.

The problem of finding the optimal allocation of rights is really one of cost-benefit analysis, which turns out to be very complicated. It would be nice to find one simple liability rule that did the

---

[1] The term 'bribe' is used to describe a monetary payment made by one person to persuade another to change his behaviour. It does not necessarily denote criminal behaviour in this context.

trick and indeed both Posner [*13*] and Demsetz [*5*] argue that 'fault' may be an approximate solution. Thus, 'A deeper analysis of these precedents [set by Court judgments] may reveal that they generally make sense from the economic viewpoint of placing the liability on that party who can, at least-cost, reduce the probability of a costly interaction happening' [*5*; *2*]. This is still an open question, but in order to justify the application of the fault rule over a wide range of accident producing activities, it is necessary to show that accident rates are more sensitive to changes in the vigilance and care of human beings than to any other variable. There is no a priori reason why this should be so; the matter is an empirical one.

Whether or not tort is a compensatory system is a hotly debated issue. However, the fashionable questions, as Fletcher [*7*] reminds us, are instrumentalist and tort does redistribute wealth—it does provide compensation for some.

The fault system redistributes wealth from those whose behaviour is found not to conform to an accepted, though objective,[1] standard to those who are injured through that behaviour. It implies a set of values in which society values the income of the latter group higher than that of the former. All we can do (whilst still wearing our economists' hats) is to ask questions which we cannot answer. Does this idea of justice reflect the values of society as a whole (whatever 'as a whole' may mean)? and, if so, can we afford it? (i.e. how high are the trans-action costs?).

The fault system also redistributes the individual's spread of income over time, or different states of health, for whilst it imposes a contingent liability (of being negligent) it also bestows a contingent benefit (of being compensated for an injury because someone else has been found negligent). This is particularly apparent in those activities, such as motoring, where the same action both exposes the driver to risk and imposes risks upon other drivers. On the other hand, certain activities might be considered non-reciprocal, such as flying an aeroplane over a built-up area. Ultimately, all activities could be defined so widely as to make everything reciprocal, or so narrowly as to make nothing reciprocal. Without labouring the point at this stage,

---

[1] Behaviour is defined by reference to the 'reasonable' man. Negligence does not ask about the particular motives or perceptions of the individual.

suffice it to note that the fault system does simultaneously impose costs and benefits upon individuals which tend to redistribute their income between times of health and times of impairment.

Economic welfare theory has traditionally held that an economic system which prevents individuals from exercising their preferences over economic goods, even though they are able to bear the costs involved to society, is inefficient. One such sort of preferences might relate income in times of health and unimpaired earning capacity to income in times of disability and distress. An efficient system will allow him to transfer freely from one state to another at a rate determined by the transaction costs involved. The fault system, however, performs this type of transfer but to an extent largely beyond the control of the individual. This is not strictly true because a person can affect the contingent benefit and liability by cautious and vigilant behaviour but the extent to which this may be achieved is limited because his own behaviour is assessed in terms of an objective standard and the behaviour of others is largely beyond his control. Furthermore, there will probably be high information costs in transmitting incentives through insurance premiums. However, the value of the fault system as a source of compensation can only be adequately measured against a background of other compensation systems.

In isolation, tort would tend to reduce the financial uncertainty associated with personal injury since at least some would be able to make good their loss, in full or part, by tort recovery. But other systems do exist and it may well be that tort damage tends to increase rather than reduce financial uncertainty. The reason is that the State (in the UK) will provide basic protection to all those disabled by accident or disease at a level at least adequate to provide for subsistence.[1] If people are not specifically insured under the sickness, invalidity or industrial injuries schemes, they will qualify for supplementary benefit. In addition, at least half of those in employment will be members of an employer's sick pay scheme, which may or may not contain provision for deduction of social security benefits [14]. Whilst there will be a partial deduction from any tort award for social security benefits, there

---

[1] The introduction of earnings related benefits provides a strong element of insurance against actual loss of income as opposed to the provision of basic subsistence needs.

is a complete deduction for sick pay.[1] On the other hand, no deduction is made at all for any life or accident insurance which the injured party may have purchased. In the absence of tort damages, the amount of compensation to be received is fairly predictable, although there are still some uncertainties such as whether a potential accident will qualify for industrial injury benefit or ordinary sickness benefit. Since it is more or less known how much compensation will be received, the individual can assess its adequacy and, if he wishes, purchase insurance on the private market to supplement State and employer's benefits in accordance with his own preferences. Once tort is introduced, this sort of planning tends to break down. If insurance is not purchased, one is gambling on being under-compensated; if insurance is purchased, one is gambling on being over-compensated. The final outcome is probably more sensitive to these chance factors than to the foresight and financial planning of the individual concerned.

Of those suffering accidental injury only a small proportion will ever recover tort damages and the chances of doing so vary according to where the accident occurred. The proportion of road accident victims who receive any damages at all is probably less than 50% of reported injuries[2] and for industrial accidents it is probably less than 10% of reported accidents.[3] With respect to other accidents the situation is even less clear. Accidents in the home would rarely give rise to a tort claim but others, such as passengers killed or injured on regular airline flights, would be in a much stronger position in any action taken against the airline. There is therefore considerable variability in the distribution of compensation both between different accident categories and also between different individuals within the categories.

---

[1] Unless it is paid gratuitously, in which case the legal remedy is rather confused.

[2] In the Harris & Harz survey [8] of 90 'serious' injury victims only 38 received any damages. T. G. Ison forms a general impression that the proportion is of the order of 50% though it is not quite clear whether he would include in his base all accidents or whether he would dismiss the more trivial [9].

[3] Ison (*ibid.*) suggests a figure of 10%, but figures we have obtained on a confidential basis for a large but selective sample of one particular industry show that only 5% of reported accidents which caused absence of more than 3 days resulted in successful claims.

Court Awards

The uncertainties associated with tort do not stop here. Even when awards are made in court there still appears to be a variation between awards which cannot readily be explained in terms of differing and identifiable features of each case. We have used statistical techniques in order to see whether court awards do follow some predictable pattern which can be readily formulated or whether on the contrary awards are irregular and unpredictable. We have also had in mind the hypothesis, suggested to us by several lawyers, that a high award for monetary loss tends to be offset by a low award for non-monetary loss and vice versa. Finally, we have tried to establish at what rate future income tends to be discounted and whether this is justified in terms of actuarial or economic trends. Details of the calculations cannot be included here but some tentative conclusions are summarized below.

1. The attempt was made to isolate those factors which seemed significant. Two dimensions that appear to be dominant are the type of injury and the estimated monetary loss. We chose three classes of injury. In order to isolate the calculation of income loss, fatality cases in which dependents were left were chosen. Secondly, a comparison was made of paraplegia cases on grounds that the medical, social and economic implications of these injuries were somewhat similar between cases. For similar reasons, a selection of quadriplegia cases was also chosen. Prediction of the level of awards in other injury categories will probably be much more difficult because of the greater physical/economic heterogenity between cases,[1] and also because we wished to test the more serious cases. Finally, an independent calculation was made of the imputed rate of interest in injury cases by selecting recent cases in which the overall award was divided into its various components.

2. The rate at which future income is discounted varies considerably between death cases. The mean rate was 5.3% but for young men the rate was usually about twice this and for older

---

[1] e.g. even if say a broken leg were similar medically between two cases the implication for absence from work would differ enormously between different occupation categories.

men, it was considerably lower. Some justification could be made for discounting young men at a higher rate since the remarriage prospects of the widow used to be a relevant factor.[1] However even this contingency was insufficient to explain the differential.

3. The rate at which future income was discounted was significantly higher in injury cases (mean 7.5%) than in death cases whereas one would expect it to be lower. The 'contingencies' are similar except that remarriage is not at issue in injury cases. Even on modest assumptions about future inflation and increases in the productivity of labour, average earnings would grow in the order of 6% per annum. Without allowing for contingencies, this means that a net of tax rate of interest of about 13–14% would be necessary to produce the required income stream increasing in money terms at 6% per annum. Given the age of our sample (average about 32) it would be difficult to justify a discount rate of more than 4% for contingencies such as mortality and unemployment. This produces a 'certainty equivalent' growth of money earnings of around 2% and still a net of tax return on the award of around 9–10% would be required to produce this income stream.

4. It was difficult to provide a direct test for the hypothesis that monetary and non-monetary awards tend to offset each other: the cases which do classify the award into its components are compatible with this hypothesis but are too few to be statistically significant.

5. The paraplegia model does explain the level of awards fairly well. There is some residual variation, and it is difficult to explain this except in terms of incorrect formulation of the model. The actual and expected values were compared and then an attempt was made to explain any large divergence by referring back to the case and trying to identify any peculiar features. In some cases there were circumstances which might explain the deviation (e.g. exceptional promotion prospects, shortened life expectation, etc.) but in many other cases the deviation remained a mystery. We concluded that there was a significant degree of erratic variation between awards.

---

[1] This is not the case now. Section 4(1) of the Law Reform (Miscellaneous Provisions) Act 1971 prohibits the court from taking account of actual remarriage and remarriage prospects.

I.D.H.—3*

6. For quadreplegia cases the model was far less satisfactory in terms of its descriptive powers, and the variation between the actual and predicted value of awards was much more difficult to explain by referring back to the case to pick up factors not described in the model.

The general conclusion we drew from our limited analysis of court awards was that (*a*) they discounted the future too highly, and that (*b*) although the paraplegia model does fit well in the other cases there is a wide variation in awards which is difficult to explain in terms of identifiable features of the cases. These problems could be eased within the present framework of the law [*10*; *11*] but even if that were done, significant variations would remain.

Further analysis of court cases would throw more light on the level and adequacy of awards but it would still be dealing with a very small proportion of all cases. The vast majority, probably 95% or more, of tort claims are settled out of court. Although the ultimate threat of litigation does provide some constraint on out of court settlement the solution is found through a bargaining process. This process introduces another range of uncertainty and variation in the level of tort damages. In addition, the question of fault is not an 'all or nothing' affair and many accident victims have their damages reduced on the grounds that their own negligence had been a contributory factor in causing the accident. But even this variation is overshadowed by the selectivity of the fault principle, which results in compensation for only a minority of those suffering personal injury.

II

Compensation for personal injury is big business. Even though the numbers of people impaired through accidental injury are small in relation to those impaired through disease, they are nevertheless large in absolute numbers and the money transfers induced by injury run into hundreds of millions of pounds. Here we intend to estimate numerically the distribution of tort damages, and its associated costs and sources of finance. For analytical purposes we also need to form a picture of how compensation from other sources is distributed and comparative information is presented on social security, industrial injuries, national health and private insurance and employers' sick pay schemes.[1]

One perspective on the magnitude of the problem can be formed by looking at the numbers of people involved. Estimates are given in Table 3.1, following a division into road, industrial, home and other accidents. (This environmental division becomes useful later on.) There is a problem of non-reporting which may be quite serious especially for relatively minor accidents, and even for the more serious cases which receive hospital 'in-patient' treatment the residual 'other and unspecified' group must contain large numbers which should have been specifically allocated to the other environmental categories. The particularly interesting feature to emerge is that severity of accidents varies according to environmental circumstances: in particular road accidents produce a very much higher ratio of serious casualties and fatalities than do industrial accidents. This pattern should be borne in mind when considering the distribution of compensation between the different types of accident.

TABLE 3.1 **Personal Injuries 1970**

Type of Accident	Injuries	Numbers receiving 'in-patient' treatment in hospital	Fatalities
Road Accidents	355,847	91,920	7,501
Industrial Accidents	833,000	30,000	985
Home Accidents	n/a	104,630	7,378
Other or Unspecified	n/a	283,400	6,340

The figures in this table have been extracted or estimated from the following sources: Annual Report of the DHSS 1971; Statutory returns of Industrial accidents under the Factories Acts and other industrial legislation; Hospital In-Patient Enquiry 1969; various publications of the Royal Society for the Prevention of Accidents and the Annual Abstract of Statistics.

Estimating the aggregate tort damage paid in respect to personal injury claims is a very tricky affair and the scraps of information we have used to build up the picture range from those which are

---

[1] Some of the material in this section appeared, in slightly different form, in [12]. A fuller exposition of sources and methods of the numerical estimates has been submitted as written evidence to the Pearson Commission.

statistically impeccable to pure hunches. Although there remains a margin of error which we cannot accurately quantify we intend only to establish the general orders of magnitude. We hope to show the broad patterns which emerge in the distribution of accident compensation. We estimate below how much compensation was paid in tort damages for road, industrial and other accidents for a single year (1970) and compare this with compensation emanating from other sources. Although we give a brief description of our method of estimation for tort we do not do so for other systems. In fact many of the other estimates have required similar gymnastics and our excuse for not displaying our method is brevity.

Since third party liability for motor vehicle accidents is compulsory, the most apparent source of aggregate data on court awards for road accidents lies in insurance records. Until recently however even this source of data was difficult to tap since insurers did not usually separate underwriting results between British and foreign business. This separation is now compulsory. From insurance company returns to the Department of Trade and Industry and published material of the British Insurance Association, the total insurance claims for motor vehicle accidents in the United Kingdom appears to be about £214m. On the basis of information supplied by companies, approximately one-fifth of this relates to third party bodily injury claims and a further 2% to passenger liability claims. This gives a figure of £47m. To this should be added the payments made by the Motor Insurers Bureau[1] and claims paid by those who have been permitted to self insure by lodging deposits with the Department of Trade and Industry. This gives a total figure of tort damage payments for injuries in road accidents of around £50m in 1970.[2]

For industrial accidents we have used similar techniques though there was some problem in separating employers' liability insurance.[3] This was eventually done by taking the total liability

---

[1] This agency makes payments for personal injury claims when liability insurance is inoperative.

[2] This figure is surprisingly close to Atiyah's [1, p. 493]. This similarity in results is largely coincidental since he appears to have overestimated premiums and the relative cost of TPBI claims but underestimated the claims premium ratio.

[3] Compulsory returns now only separate UK liability insurance as a separate class for which DTI returns must be made.

insurance premium for UK and dividing these between employers' liability and other in the proportions which these sub-classes represented in the world-wide business of British insurers. The estimation was further complicated by the long delays in settling claims and specific data relating to UK 1970 claims was not available. Here we used the ratio of claims paid to premium written for world wide business to provide an estimate of about £20m for UK employers' liability claims. However, using Department of Employment data on the cost of employers' liability insurance per employee in different industries we estimate a figure in the region of £24–£26m. Furthermore, employers' liability insurance was not compulsory in 1970 and we have therefore added a further 10% to account for self insurance on the part of employers.[1] The final estimate is therefore £27.5m.

Other liability insurance would cover both personal injury claims and other forms of liability and there was virtually no data on how this may be divided. A fifty-fifty division based on the rough estimates of insurance company claims managers produces a figure of £12m, though we admit that this may contain a significant degree of error. A further £2m is added to allow for self insurance.

These estimates are now presented in Table 3.2 alongside comparative data for other compensation systems. The figures relate to net compensation paid to accident victims.

The table shows that although the classic remedy of recovering damages under common law still accounts for a large amount of compensation, it now plays only a supporting role. In aggregate terms, the State probably administers as much compensation to accident victims as the other sources put together. Also significant is the point that personal insurance, particularly for non-fatal injury cases, plays a relatively unimportant role, although life assurance is a rapidly growing form of protection. On breaking down net compensation administered by the various systems into an environmental classification of accidents, a very different pattern emerges. For road accidents, the tort system with all its vagaries and uncertainties is the dominant source of compensation, whereas industrial accident victims receive the bulk of their

---

[1] In one survey 91·3% of employers in manufacturing industries paid employers' liability premiums (6). It is not known however what proportion of the labour force is accounted for by these 91·3% of employers.

TABLE 3.2 **Compensation for Personal Injury, 1970**

Source	Road Accidents £m	Industrial Accidents £m	Other £m	Total £m
(1) Social Security Benefit				
Sickness	7·3	not applicable		
Death	4·9	„	38·7	
Supplementary	0·6	„		
Industrial Injury	not available	33·4	not applicable	
„ Disablement	„	60·6	„	
„ Death	„	8·5	„	
Total	12·8[1]	102·5[2]	38.7	154·0
(2) Tort	50·0	27·5[3]	14·0	91·5
(3) Sick pay	2·7	18·5	28·2	49·4
(4) Personal Insurance	11·6	2·2	21·8	35·6
(5) National Health	11·6	23·0	50·9	85·5
(6) Totals	88·7	173·7	153·6	416·0

Notes:
1 This figure will probably underestimate the total social security payments to road accident victims. Some accident victims will have qualified for the industrial benefits if their accidents occurred out of and in the course of their employment.
2 Payment for prescribed diseases is included but accounts for a relatively small proportion of the total.
3 These figures differ slightly from those presented by us in D. S. Lees and N. Doherty 'Compensation for Personal Injury', *Lloyds Bank Review*, April 1973. The reason is that more complete records of company returns to the Department of Trade and Industry and other data are now available.

Sources:
The figures for the industrial injury, disablement and death benefits are extracted from the Annual Report of the Department of Health and Social Security 1970. The other figures are estimates based upon data extracted from a variety of sources including annual reports of the DHSS; Annual Abstract of Statistics; the Robens Report on *Safety and Health at Work*; Hospital Costing Returns; Insurance Directory and Yearbook; *The Cost of Road Accidents in Great Britain*, by R. F. F. Dawson; DHSS Reports on Hospital In-Patient Enquiry; statutory returns made by insurance companies; Registrar Generals Statistical Reviews of England and Wales; *Fringe Benefits and Labour Costs*, by Reid and Robertson; MPNI Report of an Inquiry into the Incidence of Incapacity for Work; and various publications by the British Insurance Association and the Royal Society for the Prevention of Accidents.

compensation from the State under the industrial injuries scheme. The implication is that compensation for industrial accidents is much more widely distributed and is more closely related to the actual losses suffered by the victims. For the residual group, the tort recovery is probably explained by non-road transport accidents and the liability of property owners to the public. Those who suffer accidents in the home (possibly the largest single group of accident victims) do not qualify for the industrial injury benefit nor are the circumstances of their accident likely to give rise to a tort claim. Thus apart from personal insurance or sick pay they have to rely on sickness or supplementary benefits.

Perhaps the most startling contrast between the various compensation systems is to be made on the basis of their respective administrative or transfer costs. The particularly interesting feature is the extremely high cost of administering the tort system. This arises (a) because it is under-pinned by a system of liability insurance which itself is extremely costly to administer, and (b) because the determination of liability and the assessment of damages in each individual case are such complex issues that their resolution demands much time and expense from insurers and lawyers as well as the direct parties to the action. The dominant costs are incurred even before the incidents which give rise to the tort claim take place: namely, the costs of under-writing and managing a system of liability insurance. One estimate sets these costs alone at 80% of the net compensation administered [9] and other costs associated with actual claims at a further 22.3%. Our own estimate of the insurance costs is rather lower since we do not include insurers' profit. The largest branch of liability insurance, motor insurance, has run at a considerable loss over the past few years: this does not indicate a reduction in transfer costs but rather that motor insurance is being subsidized by other policyholders and/or shareholders of the insurance companies. Our own estimate[1] is that insurance costs amount to 51.8% to which we have added the 22.3% for other costs giving a total ratio of transfer costs to net benefits administered of about 74%.

---

[1] Based upon data extracted from the Insurance Directory and Yearbook 1970/71/72; data published by the British Insurance Association, and insurance company accounts filed with the Department of Trade and Industry.

In contrast to tort, the transfer costs associated with the other compensation system are considerably lower. For sickness benefit they are considerably less than 10% of net benefits administered and for industrial injury benefit are probably in the order of 15%.[1] Private life issurance has transfer costs of about 15–18% of benefits, personal accident insurance 55% and employers' sick pay schemes probably less than 10%. Admittedly the social functions of the various schemes may differ, but the implication might be drawn that 'justice', as an element in tort, is an expensive commodity.

We now look at the distribution of the financial burden of supporting the compensation system. Table 3.3 shows who pays

TABLE 3.3   Sources of Finance for Compensation Systems, 1970

	General and Local Taxation	Employer	Employee	At Risk	Motorists
	£m	£m	£m	£m	£m
(a) **Road Accidents**					
Social Security[1] Benefit	1·8	Flat 4·3	Flat 3·9	—	—
Supplementary	0·6	Grad. 1·5	Grad. 1·5	—	—
National Health	9·2	0·3	0·7	—	—
Personal Insurance	—	—	—	13·6	—
Tort	—	—	—	—	87·0
Sick Pay	—	2·8	—	—	—
	11·6	8·9	6·1	13·6	87·0
(b) **Industrial Accidents**					
Social Security Industrial Injuries	17·2	50·5	36·1	—	—
National Health	19·8	0·7	1·4	—	—
Personal Insurance	—	—	—	3·0	—
Tort	—	48·0	—	—	—
Sick Pay	—	19·4	—	—	—
	37·0	118·6	37·5	3·0	Not applicable

Notes:
The date is derived from the sources referred to earlier in this section. The aggregate of these figures is equal to net compensation plus transfer costs.
1   Social security contributions are divided into flat rate (unrelated to income) and graduated (related to income).

[1] These figures include estimates of the costs of collection borne by employers.

for the compensation systems and in what capacity. Thus, for example, the bulk of compensation for road accidents is paid for by motorists in the form of insurance premiums, but some is provided by taxpayers in the form of subsidies to the social security and health services and by employers and employees. The category 'at risk' shows the insurance contributions of those who buy personal insurance which includes, but is not limited to, road accidents or industrial accidents.

If internalization of costs is a matter of social justice, then it is interesting to note that the compensation systems limit the bulk of their costs to those groups who are involved in, or exposed to, the risk of accidents. The categories 'motorists' and 'at risk' together with victims themselves bear the bulk of the costs of road accidents, and since these groups overlap considerably with taxpayers and employees, then motorist and pedestrians will in effect pay nearly all the costs. Similarly in the case of industrial accidents, employers and employees either in these roles or wearing their taxpayers' hats will be paying the compensation bill for industrial accidents. But internalization of costs is not a sufficient criterion.

A significant proportion of the compensation revenue is raised in such a way as to provide no direct incentives for motorists, employers or potential accident victims to consider the social costs of their activities. With motoring, the individual's tax or social security assessment is independent of the number of miles he drives or the way in which he drives them. Similarly, the relationship between general taxation assessment for an individual or a firm and those factors which determine the frequency and severity of industrial accidents must be very roundabout indeed. Tort, on the other hand, does provide incentives for employers, motorists, etc., to make adjustments in their level of activity and in the standard of safety but, as we have already pointed out, the particular division of cost imposed by negligence is somewhat arbitrary and is also dependent upon insurance underwriting procedures.

Whilst tort does account for a large percentage of compensation of road accidents, its relative importance is less in the case of other accidents. If reform is to provide the appropriate types of incentives for regulating accidents, other than those occurring on the road, it is particularly important that it should not be confined to tort.

III

Although the case for reform has in most instances been based upon the inadequacies of the compensatory function of the fault system, the economic approach discussed here suggests that regulatory functions are also important. We have adopted a broad classification of reform proposals which comprises strict liability, no fault and the comprehensive fund.

The approach adopted in Section I was that the regulatory function was best performed by allocating costs to the most efficient cost avoider. This term has two dimensions. It refers both to the sensitivity of accident rates to changes in the behaviour of the actors involved and to the costs involved in inducing such behavioural changes. We have already looked at the proposition that accident rates might be more sensitive to vigilance and care than to any other simple basis for a liability rule. A prima facie case can be made against the fault system on the grounds that costs of inducing changes in behaviour are extremely high.

There does appear to be a general case for a strict liability approach where certain conditions are present. Where a large degree of risk is concentrated upon a small and identifiable group of people the law has usually been prohibitive. Tort on the other hand has had a regulatory function in those situations in which accidents occur somewhat randomly over a large group commonly exposed to risk. The activity with which the accidents are associated relates two groups of people: those whose decisions determine the manner and extent of the activity and those who are exposed to its side effects, namely accidental injury. In the case of an activity such as motoring these groups are indistinguishable but for many other activities the groups are not only separate but decisions concerning the manner and extent of the activity are highly centralized.[1] Examples are readily apparent: an employer with a large labour force, an airline and those beneath its flight paths (or even its passengers), the industrialist

---

[1] It has been argued that if there is a contractual relationship between the parties involved the allocation of costs is immaterial (16; 5).

who undertakes some factory process with high fire/explosion risk thereby exposing passers-by and neighbours to risk of injury, or producers of a potentially dangerous consumer product. In examples of this kind, the allocation of costs to the party who makes decisions on output, production, activity level, etc., appears to be the most efficient. To this group accident costs will appear as a fairly regular cost of the activity and the employer (or whoever) is in a position to relate decisions concerning safety to decisions concerning other costs and benefits of the activity. For the employee, however, the prospect of an accident is little more than a remote fear and this provides a very imperfect indicator of the degree of care needed by him to relate the risk of accident to other costs and benefits of his work effort.

The question of centralization of decisions is also important in the context of negotiation between the parties. Collective bargaining between unions and employers does lead to changes in safety standards but the process is not without its costs. In many other cases however the population at risk is either widely dispersed (those beneath the aviation lines) or perhaps only in temporary association (passengers in a train) such that the prospect of collective bargaining becomes remote.

In contrast, other types of accident-producing activities are governed by atomistic decision making and the group which makes these decisions becomes superimposed on that which is at risk. Motoring is the obvious example. The rationale of the strict liability approach is that these two groups are separable and it becomes meaningless when they are not. The fault system has created another categorization of those involved, which has focussed not on particular activities but on particular accidents. The actors are separated according to their behavioural relationships with each other which culminate in the accident. 'No fault'[1] in contrast sub-divides no further than those involved in the activities to which it applies. For collisions between motorists, the costs are left to 'lie as they fall' and the law imposes no redistribution between those involved. This is usually accom-

---

[1] 'No fault' appears to be used in two different connections. In a general context it is used to describe alternatives to the fault system (including strict liability) but in a specific sense it is applied to reforms in which each shall pay for his own loss and usually shall be required to insure against such loss.

panied by compulsory insurance and the scope of the no fault scheme may be such that negligence is completely displaced (the Woodhouse Scheme [15]) or is displaced for losses below some prescribed ceiling (as in most North American schemes).

A switch to 'no fault' would imply changes in the behavioural incentives to those involved. For example, the careful driver might be expected to be a net beneficiary under a negligence system in the sense that for any accident in which he might become involved it is more likely that he will recover from the other party than pay damages to that other party. No fault will therefore increase the cost of accidents for this group and thus provides incentives to drive fewer miles and to do so even more carefully. The other side of the coin is that hitherto careless drivers will be induced to drive more miles and the penalty on their lack of care will be relaxed. There are two open questions here. Firstly, the overall impact on accident rates depends upon the relative sensitivity of the two groups to financial incentives and in the manner in which these incentives may be transmitted through insurance premiums. This is a subject worthy of specific research as no general case can be made in favour of either system. Secondly a switch to no fault would also involve redistributions of wealth between these two groups[1] and this calls for a conscious examination of the values implicit in our notion of 'justice'.

The philosophy of the Woodhouse Scheme for New Zealand is that distinctions between environmental causes of accidents or the occupational status of the victims are irrelevant to compensation. The Report explicitly rejects a system of merit rating largely on the basis of assertions that the deterrent effects of financial penalties are insignificant or unimportant [15, paras. 328–336].

In terms of the compensatory function, those reforms which: (a) reduce the uncertainty associated with the distribution of

---

[1] There might also be wealth redistributions between different income groups. Negligence implies a contingent liability which will be determined in part by the incomes of other participants in the activity. The contingent benefit in tort is however related to that income of the actor involved. Under no fault however the loss/benefit effects of accidents are independent of incomes of other participants.

compensation; (*b*) increase the sensitivity of the distribution of compensation to individual choice or social values or (*c*) which reduce the transaction costs associated with the distribution of compensation, are to be encouraged. In terms of the reforms considered these are, to some extent, competing objectives. Some of the strongest pressure for 'no fault' for activities such as motoring has been based upon the observation that it costs approximately one dollar in administration to administer one dollar of compensation. This consideration has led to a predominance of 'no fault' schemes which are publicly operated and which provide compulsory cover up to some defined ceiling: the normal tort claims can be pursued for higher damages. The argument in favour of a state fund is that it is considerably cheaper to operate and the cost comparisons which we made in Section II appear to suggest similar proposals for the UK. To what extent the cheapness of the State schemes is due to the compulsory nature of the cover and to what extent it is due to its insulation from certain types of costs borne by private insurers (advertising costs, agency commissions, etc.) is a little unclear. To some extent however the low transaction costs are due to the homogeneity of cover and the standardization of benefits and correspondingly there is some sacrifice of consumer choice. On the other hand some minimum level of state benefit to accident victims or anyone else deprived of income may correspond with the government's distributional objectives. It is impossible to unscramble the effects of the distributional objective and convenience of standardized cover which are implied in a given ceiling for compulsory cover. In implementing a no fault scheme the relevant questions are . . . 'what level of compulsory cover balances the sacrifice of consumer choice with the reduction in administrative costs?' and 'how is this level of compulsory cover affected by the government's distributional objective?'

Apart from these issues the 'no fault' approach must reduce some of the financial uncertainty associated with accidental injury. The value of compensation for given types of accidents is readily determinable and does not rest on contingencies such as the proof of negligence or the degree of negligence. In these circumstances the individual can more easily assess his insurance needs. Even if there is compulsory cover the compensation paid to the accident victim is sensitive at the margin to his own demands for insurance protection. Under a system of negligence the residual compensation, over and above any state sickness, etc. benefit is determined largely by random factors.[1]

The argument that compulsory 'no fault' insurance can operate at low administrative costs appears to be eminently plausible although ultimately only experience and empirical testing will show whether this is so. A priori, it would be much more difficult to rationalize that a move from negligence to strict liability would lead to any significant effects on administrative costs. Whilst it is true that the liability issue would be simplified from one of determining negligence to one of determining causation, a switch to strict liability does not reduce the need for liability insurance, which bulks large in administrative costs.

Although it may be useful to discriminate between different accident producing activities when considering the allocation of resources and the regulation of accidents, it is not apparent that this should be the case when considering the distribution of compensation. A person's needs are not different if he is paraplegic through an accident on the roads or an accident at work. Nor is it apparent that the collective sympathy felt by the community, and for which it is willing to pay compensation, is any greater in the one case than in the other. Whilst it may be true that the chances of injury may be greater when using the roads than travelling in a train, it is difficult to see how this could affect the amount of compensation one would require if an accident should occur. It may mean that one is willing to pay a higher premium for protection against road accidents than rail accidents.

Conclusion

Although the functions of the tort of negligence are rarely made explicit (and when they are there is little agreement) it would seem

---

[1] A further factor relevant to policy making which we do not consider here is the delay in the settlement of claims. In terms of US 'no fault' proposals this point has been important. The delay in settling claims would be irrelevant in terms of our welfare criteria if interest payment were made and if unlimited borrowing and lending were available at the market rate of interest. Where there are market imperfections the delay can have important welfare implications. On the other hand the social security arrangements in the UK reduce at least some of the pressure for immediate damages for accident victims.

that the compensatory function is constrained by the competing functions of deterring accidents and providing justice as between individuals. The conflict of functions results, among other things, in considerable discrimination in the distribution of damages, high transaction costs and often long delays in the making of awards. It is these features, together with uncertainties of settlement in individual cases, that have provoked widespread and sustained hostility against the fault system. The results reported herein on fault as a method of determining and distributing compensation in the United Kingdom tend to support the critics.

But compensation is not the only issue. Regulation of accidents is of comparable social importance. If the fault system is to be replaced, its successor should embody incentives for accident avoidance, which the fault system contains, though the precise effects have yet to be estimated. In practice, many proposals for reform have ignored these incentives. In addition, fault implies a highly decentralized set of arrangements, requiring a minimum of detailed control by government, while alternative schemes are highly centralized and typically financed by compulsory contributions. Loss of flexibility and individual freedom of choice, while less readily quantifiable, must also be weighed in the balance.

References

1. Atiyah, P. S., *Accidents, Compensation and the Law*, London, Weidenfeld & Nicholson, 1970 (p. 493)

2. Blum, W. J. and Kalven, H. Jnr., 'The Empty Cabinet of Dr Calabresi'—Auto Accidents and General Deference, *University of Chicago Law Review*, Vol. 34, 1967

3. Calabresi, G., *The Cost of Accidents: A Legal and Economic Analysis*, London, New Haven, 1970

4. Coase, R. H., 'The Problem of Social Cost', 3, *Journal of Law and Economics*, 1, 1960

5. Demsetz, H., 'When does the rule of liability matter?', *Journal of Legal Studies*, Vol. 1 (1) January 1972

6. Department of Employment, *Survey of Labour Costs 1968*, London, HMSO, 1971

7. Fletcher, G. P., 'Fairness and Utility in Tort Theory', *Harvard Law Review*, Vol. 85, No. 3, January 1972 (p. 538)

8. Harris, D. R. and Harz, S., *Report of a Pilot Survey of the Financial*

Consequences of Personal Injuries suffered in Road Accidents in the City of Oxford 1968. Unpublished report, Oxford, 1968

9. Ison, T. G., *The Forensic Lottery*, London, Staples Press, 1967

10. Law Commission, *Working Papers No. 27 and 41 First Programme Item VIB*, 'Personal Injury Litigation: Assessment of Damages', London, The Law Commission, 1970/71

11. Law Commission, *No. 56 Report on Personal Injury Litigation—Assessment of Damages*, HC 373, London, HMSO, 1973

12. Lees, D. S. and Doherty, N., 'Compensation for Personal Injury', *Lloyds Bank Review*, April 1973

13. Posner, R. A., 'A Theory of Negligence', *Journal of Legal Studies*, Vol. I (1) January 1972

14. Reid, G. L. and Robertson, D. J., *Fringe Benefits, Labour Costs: Social Security*, London, Allen and Unwin, 1964

15. Royal Commission of Enquiry, *Compensation for Personal Injury—New Zealand*. Report of the Royal Commission of Inquiry (Woodhouse Report), Wellington, New Zealand, 1967

16. Williamson, O. E., Olson, D. G. and Ralston, A., 'Externalities Insurance Disability Analysis', *Economics*, August 1967

2

DETAILED STUDIES

Introduction

The following six chapters represent specific attempts to measure and assess aspects of the cost of impairment from a wide variety of angles. In spite of the diversity of approach, however, the chapters fall naturally into three pairs—each pair relating to a common theme.

Chapters 4 and 5, by Akehurst and Dawson respectively, deal broadly with two sources of disability, the highly specialized case of asbestosis resulting from handling asbestos, and the widespread case of road traffic accidents. Both chapters are concerned with the problems and costs of controlling these sources of disability, and are to some extent complementary. For example, Dawson goes into a fair degree of detail about the subjective costs of accidents, while Akehurst prefers to leave these out of the account of his study, which is still in its early stages.

Chapters 6 and 7 both describe research projects aimed at evaluating the relative costs of home and hospital care for two very different categories of disabled people—'responauts' (polio patients at least partially dependent on artificial respiration) and mentally ill patients. They reveal shared problems, such as the need for support of families to enable home care to be effective, and differences, such as the special physical requirements of the responauts and their need for hospital back-up services.

The last two chapters in this section are concerned with problems of classifying disability, and in the case of Garrad, with its definition. Scientific investigation cannot proceed without appropriate taxonomies; we cannot indeed even assess the prevalence of disability and weigh out the apples until we know how to distinguish between apples and pears, and these efforts to refine and utilize classifications are therefore of fundamental importance. The paper that Rosser and Watts originally gave at the conference contained a second section on the use of their classification system to analyse the consistency of awards made by the courts in personal injury cases. The interest at the conference was, however, so sharply focussed on the classification categories themselves and their use to measure the outcome of treatment that the second part was barely touched on and has not therefore been reproduced here. This indicates that there is a real need for an adequate classification of degrees of disability at the practical level.

4 Regulating the Use of Asbestos[1]

R. L. *AKEHURST*

Asbestos is the generic term for a variety of hydrated silicate minerals which have in common the ability to be separated into relatively soft, silky fibres. The name is applicable to all minerals which fit this description.

There are two main classes of asbestos, differing in their crystal structures: serpentine and amphiboles. The sole member of the serpentine class is chrysotile asbestos. This is by far the most important form, accounting for more than 90% of the asbestos fibre produced. The commercially important forms of amphibole asbestos are crocidolite, amosite and anthophyllite. Physical and chemical properties differ widely between types of asbestos so it is by no means certain that the biological effects of one variety of asbestos will be mimicked by another.

Asbestos is used widely in industry, but the main uses can be summarized as: brake linings, clutch facings and other friction materials; asbestos cement products; yarns and fabrics; thermal and acoustic insulation products; and packings and seals.

Certain diseases are believed to be associated with exposure to asbestos dust and I propose briefly to review the evidence for the nature of the associations.

Asbestosis

Asbestosis, the one mineral pneumoconiosis that has been increasing in recent years, is a form of pulmonary fibrosis.

[1] Acknowledgment is made to the Medical Research Council and the Asbestosis Research Council for grants made to the Institute of Social and Economic Research, University of York.

Symptoms of the disease are breathlessness on exertion, cough and 'tightness' in the chest. Other features of the disease are clubbing of the fingers, cyanosis (restricted chest movement), kyphosis (loss of height), and fine rales heard over the lung bases. The signs become more frequent and marked as the disease progresses and when definite signs of right heart failure appear the men are unable to work and are unlikely to survive the next acute respiratory illness. A majority of individuals are susceptible to asbestosis [3]. If people are exposed to high enough concentrations of asbestos dust or are exposed for a long time, a majority will develop asbestosis. Furthermore, the disease progresses after removal from the dust, and workers can develop the disease after they have changed jobs.

Work by Knox and associates [5] and the British Occupational Hygiene Society [1] (BOHS) provided experience on which an assessment of the dangers of exposure to asbestos was made. The BOHS, on the basis of a survey of 290 men exposed in an asbestos textile factory, calculated the statistical relationship between cumulative exposure to asbestos dust (measured as the product of dust concentration and years exposed) to the prevalence of asbestosis as indicated by the presence of basal rales, the earliest sign to appear.

Bronchogenic Cancer

Although it was realized in the 1920s that asbestos exposure could lead to fibrosis of the lung, it was not until 1947 that the possibility of asbestos fibre causing cancer was seriously considered. The reason for this was that government regulations introduced in 1931 had to a great extent stopped the really massive exposures to asbestos dust that were common before then. This meant that men did not die quickly of asbestosis, as they had earlier, but lived long enough to develop lung cancer. So the higher incidence of cancer deaths was partly a consequence, ironically, of improved hygiene standards.

Evidence on the relationship between the cumulative exposure and the incidence of the disease is not as good in the case of lung cancer as it is in the case of asbestosis. What evidence there is suggests that incidence increases with level of exposure, but no quantitative estimate has been made of the relationship. One problem here is the length of time which elapses between exposure and development of the disease (a minimum of 16 years and an average of between 25 and 30 years). Consequently, we need to know dust levels in factories 25 years ago and relate these to morbidity experience now if we are to obtain an estimate of the relationship.

A study by Newhouse [6] probably gives the best guidance to the relationship between level of industrial exposure and incidence of lung cancer. She examined the mortality records of 4,500 workers employed at an asbestos factory, splitting them up by type of job. A rating of the grade of exposure was applied to each job varying from 1—very low exposure for office workers and the like—to 6 very heavy exposure. Significant excess mortalities were found for lung cancer only in grades 5 and 6, the most severely exposed.

Mesothelioma

The third disease associated with asbestos dust exposure is mesothelioma—tumours of the peritoneal and pleural mesothelium. Very little is known of the nature of the relationship, but it is believed that crocidolite asbestos is much more dangerous in this respect than other forms of asbestos. There appears to be evidence of people developing mesothelioma after only a very short exposure to asbestos (although the tumour is very rare in the complete absence of asbestos), so response may not be dose-related. Fortunately, this tumour is rare and is swamped in terms of numbers affected by asbestosis and bronchogenic cancer, but reduction of exposures to very low levels may not affect the incidence of this disease. We simply cannot say. Newhouse [6] included mesothelioma cases in her study and this is the only remotely usable evidence.

In summary, of the evidence on the diseases we can say that we have a reasonable basis for estimating the likely effect of a reduction in dust exposure on the incidence of asbestosis, a poor but just usable basis for lung cancer, and no basis for mesothelioma.

Legislation

As mentioned earlier, regulations controlling the use of asbestos were first introduced in 1931. However, the coverage of the regulations was inadequate and, as the use of asbestos expanded in industry, progressively more workers using asbestos were not protected by the 1931 regulations. Even in the industries where the regulations did apply the standards imposed came to be regarded as inadequate. In the face of a growing body of evidence on the effects of asbestos dust exposure, new regulations controlling the use of asbestos were brought into force in May 1970. On the basis of the work done by BOHS [1] the standard set was that workers should not be exposed to a dust concentration of more than 2 fibres/cc of asbestos. On the assumption of a 50-year working life/an asbestos worker would have a cumulative exposure of 100 fibres years/cc, which implies a 1% risk of contracting asbestosis. It was assumed that the excess risk of contracting lung cancer would be reduced correspondingly.

When the 1970 Regulations were introduced the poor state of knowledge of the effects of asbestos exposure was acknowledged, and it was stated that these Regulations might be revised in the light of further information. The level at which the regulations were fixed was to a large extent arbitrarily chosen, based on the idea that a 1% risk of asbestosis was the 'right' level. It was felt, however, by some of the people involved in setting the level, that the process was too arbitrary and that fuller study was called for.

Accordingly, I set out to try to calculate the 'right' level, or at least to expose what was involved in choosing some particular level. In principle, choosing the optimum level for regulations is simple—examine how the marginal costs of changing the dust level by a small amount vary with the absolute dust level, do the same with the marginal benefits, find the level at which the marginal costs equal the marginal benefits and that is the optimum. In practice, of course, the conceptual and practical problems involved are massive. The former are inescapable, but the latter may be limited a little by an appropriate choice of exactly what is to be attempted. Accordingly, it was decided that in the first instance the study would be limited to examining the costs and benefits to be expected from the introduction of the 1970 Regulations, and the effects of any small divergences from the maximum permitted dust level set in those Regulations.

Likely effect of the 1970 Regulations

I propose here to restrict the scope of the discussion even further to keep it within reasonable bounds. I am therefore concentrating on examining what is required to estimate the likely effect of the 1970 Regulations. All of the conceptual problems and most of the practical problems that are to be encountered in a fuller study are illustrated here.

Before discussing the nature and measurement of the costs and benefits to be derived from introducing the Regulations, one assumption has to be made explicit. It is assumed that dust levels decided upon will actually be enforced. Bearing in mind the size of the factory inspectorate, and the difficulties involved in tracking down the end uses of asbestos, this may not be the case, but problems of enforcement are assumed away.

Identification and measurement of the likely benefits of the introduction of the Regulations

When a workman is exposed to asbestos dust and as a consequence contracts a related disease, a number of costs are involved. These will be enumerated presently. The benefit to be gained from the introduction of the Regulations lies in the lessening or removal of these costs. Clearly then our estimate of the benefit from the introduction of the Regulations will depend on the reduction in the number of people expected to contract an asbestos-related disease in the future and our valuation of the costs of contracting an asbestos related disease.

In order to estimate the expected reduction in the number of people who will contract asbestosis or an asbestos-related cancer we require estimates of:

(i) The number of people we expect to be exposed to asbestos dust in the future.

(ii) The dust levels which would have reigned in the absence of regulations, and the length of exposures.

(iii) The relationship between exposure to the dust and the incidence of asbestos-related disease.

Taking (i) we find a number of difficulties. First, because of the nature of the uses of asbestos it is not easy to estimate the number of people involved with asbestos at any one time. The most comprehensive estimate available was published by the Factory Inspectorate [2] for the year 1963. They estimated that about 20,000 people were then involved directly in working with asbestos. This figure did not include those persons exposed by reason of working near where asbestos is manipulated, rather than by using it directly themselves. Although this may be a source of error, the 1970 Regulations exclude people not directly involved from working near where asbestos is being used. The Factory Inspectorate estimate may therefore be taken as a reasonable starting base for projection.

We also have to project how this population will change over time. The major producers of asbestos products in the UK have expressed their willingness to supply information on their employment of workers in recent years and their projected future needs of manpower. However, these firms only account for some 60% of total employment in asbestos-using jobs, and even if the coverage were 100%, manpower forecasting is fraught with difficulties and uncertainties. Consequently, some allowance has to be made for uncertainties in the estimate.

Finally, to estimate the number of people exposed rather than the size of the population in any given year we need to know the rate of turnover and re-entry into the industry, e.g. if turnover is 40% per year and population is 20,000 then the actual number of people who have been exposed in any year is 28,000 assuming no re-entry. The major asbestos-good producers have also expressed their willingness to supply information on labour turnover and re-entry, and, subject to the limitations of coverage mentioned above, this will enable estimates to be made of the future exposed population.

Turning to (ii) above, we find that we need to estimate the length and level of exposure to asbestos dust. To estimate lengths of exposure we need to know the distribution of the length of stay of workers in jobs in the asbestos industry. Averages are useless here. The average length of stay might be, say, 5 years. For this length of time an exposure of even 20 fibres/cc would be considered 'reasonable' by BOHS. However, an average length of stay of 5 years will conceal some people who work 3 months with asbestos and others who work 30 or 40 years, and clearly high exposure for long periods will lead to risk of disease which is not 'reasonable' for part of the population. Consideration of the whole distribution of lengths of stay rather than averages will lead to different predictions about incidence of the diseases.

Estimating the levels of dust exposure that would be expected in the absence of the regulations causes difficulties also. The assumption made here is that in the absence of the regulations the dust levels would continue at their pre-regulation levels, but these levels are not well known. Some data are published, but these probably relate to the extreme cases. There are dust counts for the naval dockyard at Devonport, published in a report by Harris [4] and counts for a factory at Rochdale published by BOHS [1]. The range of counts is, however, demoralizing, ranging from well over 1,000 fibres/cc in Devonport to about 4 fibres/cc in parts of the Rochdale factory. It is probable that typical counts for the insulation industry before the regulations approximated those in the dockyard, while those in manufacturing industry are nearer those at Rochdale. Both the asbestos firms themselves and the Factory Inspectorate have declined to release such information as they have on dust counts so recourse has to be made to a great extent to the opinions of industry 'experts' as a guide to pre-regulation dust levels.

Once the number of men exposed, dust counts and length of stay in the industry are known, the savings in incidence of the diseases can be calculated provided we know the relationship between cumulative exposure and incidence—the subject of (iii) above. As indicated above, the data on which estimates of these relationships have to be based are not good. In the case of meso-thelioma, widespread agreement may not even be obtainable on the *nature* of the relationship, let alone its quantitative dimension. However, we have to make do with what we find, and the BOHS [1] and Newhouse [6] studies provide some basis for estimating the expected incidence of the diseases in the absence of and after the introduction of the 1970 Regulations.

Once the number of cases of asbestosis and lung cancer that the Regulations are expected to avoid have been calculated, these cases have to be valued. What is required is some estimate of the cost of a lung cancer death, or of a case of asbestosis. The costs arising from asbestosis-related diseases fall into three categories:

(1) Those arising from people who become ill having to have treatment.

(2) Those arising from people who become ill being unable to work.

(3) Those arising from the disability *per se* of those who have asbestosis, or from the premature death of those who contract an asbestos-related disease.

I.D.H.—4

Devonport dockyard survey

As absolutely nothing was known about those costs arising in any of these categories an attempt was made to obtain some of the relevant information by means of a survey in the naval dockyard at Devonport. The survey aimed at finding out the differences, if any, between a group of asbestotics and their controls in respect of their direct use of resources because of ill health and their time off work.

Devonport dockyard was chosen as the site for the survey for two reasons. First, there were known to be many men in the dockyard who had been exposed to asbestos in their work, and a number had been certified as disabled due to asbestosis by the Pneumoconiosis Medical Panel (PMP). In addition, surveys had been made of the dockyard population before, for different reasons, which meant that the population was well documented. Dockyard workers certified disabled due to asbestosis since 1966 were ascertained from dockyard records and age-matched controls, believed not to have been exposed to asbestos, were chosen from a 1966 dockyard population. Each subject and control was interviewed by the Medical Research Council Pneumoconiosis Unit Medical Social Worker, who filled in a questionnaire for each man concerning illness and medical treatment around the time of the subject's original acceptance by the PMP. For convenience the relevant time was taken as the year of acceptance and one year either side. In addition the GP and hospital records were obtained for both subjects and controls.

Information was obtained for the relevant three years in each case on:

(1) Treatment and care of all kinds at home whether from GPs, District Nurses or Social Workers, or relatives and friends.

(2) Care away from home: visits to GP, hospital visits as in- or out-patient, visits to clinics, ambulance trips and convalescent homes.

(3) Use of drugs.

(4) Time off work.

(5) Changes of job because of ill health.

(6) Premature retirement.

I do not propose to go into details here, but differences were found in visits to and from GPs, use of drugs, time off work while in employment, changes in job because of ill health, and premature retirement. But knowing the physical differences is clearly not enough and values have to be placed on those differences. There are no problems of principle in valuing extra GP visits or extra use of drugs, but how one should value lost earnings through changing jobs, time off work and premature retirement is a subject that cannot properly be treated here.

The information collected in Devonport related only to asbestotics. What of the costs of asbestos-related cancers? Very little is known about the cost of identifying a case of lung cancer or mesothelioma. Even the Department of Health and Social Security Committee on Smoking and Health, when approached, replied that no such figures were available despite the fact that the Committee is concerned with obtaining such figures. Some general observations can be made, however, on the likely costs of treatment and work loss in the case of the asbestos-related cancers. These costs are likely, in fact, to be low: first, because time from diagnosis of the cancer to death is very short—even in the case of current asbestos workers who are X-rayed annually, men who showed no trace of tumour on an X-ray have died of mesothelioma before the next one; secondly because the prognosis is so poor; and thirdly, because of the long time taken for the cancer to appear, workmen are often retired. The last point should not be taken to mean that we should value retired people at zero, but when considering these particular categories of cost the fact that people are often retired is relevant. The picture that emerges, then, in the case of the cancers is different from that in the case of asbestosis. In the latter case, typically, the sufferer lives for many years after onset of the disease, usually working normally at first, then perhaps changing his job and taking increasing sick leave, and finally becoming so disabled that work is impossible. In the case of the cancers the onset of the disease is typically followed fairly quickly by death.

Although these observations may be of help in making any estimates of the costs of the cancers, they are clearly poor substitutes for evidence. However, at the moment nothing can be done but record its absence.

Estimating the costs of disability *per se* and the value of a life in this kind of study is very difficult, not least because it is felt—

and perhaps rightly so—that these are the costs that weigh the most heavily. However, a full discussion of the possible approaches to estimation here would probably take up the entire conference, and I therefore propose to discuss these problems no further now, but simply record that in the full study they will receive considerable attention.

Some indication has then been made of the way in which the benefits from the introduction of the Regulations might be calculated; and the difficulties of estimating the number of cases of disease we might expect to avoid and the valuing of those cases have been pointed out. We turn now to the costs of introducing the regulations—the costs of reducing the incidence of asbestos-related disease.

There are as many detailed sources of these costs as there are uses of asbestos, literally thousands. However, methods of reducing dust exposure can be split into two broad categories and these categories can help in attempting to identify the costs.

(1) The first method involves removing the use of asbestos in achieving the end to which an original asbestos-product was put. This may mean simply substituting a new fibre for asbestos in an existing process or it may mean switching to a completely different type of product. An example of the latter would arise if local authorities ceased to buy asbestos cement sewer pipes and bought only steel or clay pipes.

(2) The second method involves producing the same end product, complete with asbestos, but taking steps to protect the workers to the level required. This protection may take the form of improved ventilation of dusty machinery, protective clothing and masks, or a change in the productive process itself. An example of the latter is the production of asbestos cloth by the Fortex method. In this case the old product, asbestos cloth, is still produced, but the process by which it is produced is much less dusty. There is an added bonus here in that the cloth produced is also less dusty so dust levels are reduced for the consumers of the cloth as well as the producers.

Clearly, these two categories are interdependent. Consumers may only switch from previously price-competitive asbestos products when they find either that the price of the good has gone up because cost increases due to the Regulations have been passed on by the producer, or because the consumers themselves find the costs of health precautions are too great to make the asbestos product worth buying.

Considering first the costs of substituting other products for asbestos products, it is important to note that these costs may not simply be pecuniary. The substitutes for asbestos may themselves be hazardous to health—this may be particularly true of fibres made by man to have similar properties to asbestos; they may behave like asbestos, but not be called asbestos and therefore not be covered by regulations. The substituting of other products for asbestos products might have consequences for technical efficiency which in turn affect life and limb. Alternative materials for braking systems in cars might be used which lead to an increase in the number of road accidents. Even a small proportionate increase in the number of accidents might wipe out any lives saved in asbestos factories.

Two sets of businesses need to be approached to find out the costs of substitution—producing firms and consuming firms. Unfortunately, the major producing firms do not wish to reveal the sales information which might enable an estimate of the size of these costs to be made. Published sales information is insufficient as it does not enable distinction to be made between changes which were due to the Regulations to be distinguished from changes due to the whole complex of factors which influence the demand for a product. The situation is made worse by the fact that the asbestos industry is to a considerable extent vertically integrated, i.e. the manufacturers often own their customers, so if the manufacturers refuse to provide information under a particular heading so do many of the customers.

There are a few independent large customers, however. The most important are the Admiralty, the Central Electricity Generating Board, and British Rail. The Admiralty has declined to co-operate on the grounds that it has no useful information, the CEGB are an unknown quantity, and British Rail have offered to help, but little data have so far been obtained.

Turning to the costs of protecting the workers directly, the situation is a little more hopeful. The major manufacturers (and some of their owned customers) are prepared to provide information on the costs of installing new ventilation equipment, the costs of running it, the costs of protective clothing, the costs of altering processes, etc. If this information can be supplemented by data from insulation work then a reasonable picture of costs in this category can be formed.

A cost which follows as a consequence either of substitution or preventive measures is unemployment. If cost increases lead to a decrease in the quantity of asbestos products demanded, some redundancy may occur in both men and machinery. Firms are willing to provide information on redundancies, but a difficulty here is deciding just what proportion of these redundancies are due to the Regulations. The industry has been suffering from some contraction anyway for both cyclical and structural reasons.

Finally, we must mention one cost, the perhaps obvious one of compensation. This is not usually included in a conventional cost-benefit analysis framework as it is judged to involve only a transfer of a given product, not any increase or decrease in it. However, compensation becomes important once we consider the impact of the Regulations on particular groups in the economy, notably the asbestos workers. Compensation comes from two sources, the companies and the government. Information on payments by the latter has been obtained, but data on the payments by individual firms are sadly lacking. Very few compensation claims from firms reach Court—they are nearly all settled outside. There has been one recent exception—Central Asbestos Co was ordered to pay £85,000 compensation to a group of its recent employees and their dependents. The firms themselves are unwilling to supply figures on compensation, and the only way in which this information might be obtained would be a survey of certified asbestotics. However, this would involve the co-operation of several Pneumoconiosis Medical Panels, which might not be obtainable.

We may conclude, if asbestos is typical, that measuring the cost of human impairment in an industrial hygiene setting is dauntingly difficult. However, it is only by attempting such measurement that the data needed will be identified.

References

1. Committee on Hygiene Standards of the British Occupational Hygiene Society, 'Hygiene Standards for Chrysotile Asbestos Dust', Ann. Occupational Hygiene, 1968, Vol. 11, pp. 47–69

2. Department of Employment and Productivity, HM Factory

Inspectorate, 'Problems Arising from the Use of Asbestos', Memorandum of the Senior Medical Inspectors Advisory Panel, London, HMSO

3. Gilson, J. C., 'Asbestos Products and the Health Problem'. Paper presented to British Occupational Hygiene Society/Asbestosis Research Council Conference, Kensington, London, 18 June 1969

4. Harries, P. G., 'The Effects and Control of Diseases Associated with Exposure to Asbestos in Devonport Dockyard'. Royal Navy Clinical Research Working Party Report No. 1, Institute of Naval Medicine, Alverstoke, Gosport

5. Knox, J. F., Holmes, S., Doll, R. and Hill, I. D., 'Mortality from Lung Cancer and Other Causes Among Workers in an Asbestos Textile Factory' *British Journal of Industrial Medicine*, Vol. 25, p. 293, 1968

6. Newhouse, M. L., 'A study of the Mortality of Workers in an Asbestos Factory', *British Journal of Industrial Medicine*, Vol. 26, p. 294, 1969

5 The Cost of Human Impairment from Road Accidents[1]

R. F. F. DAWSON

Background

The Transport and Road Research Laboratory is more interested in the overall cost of accidents than in the breakdown of the total into its component parts. Costs in this context are taken to mean full economic costs and not merely the financial ones. The costs are needed for themselves, as an input into economic assessments of road schemes; they are also needed by the Laboratory to indicate areas of worthwhile research.

Although, regrettably, there are a large number of accidents in total, at any particular site or in any particular set of circumstances the numbers are small and as will be seen, the variation of costs is large. The statistic that is most commonly required is therefore, the average cost of an accident averaged over all severities. Calculations are made of the cost of fatal, serious and slight accidents and these are subdivided into accidents in urban areas, rural areas and on motorways but not according to the number or class of vehicles involved or the manoeuvre that preceded the accident.

Road accidents are frequently divided into personal injury accidents and damage only accidents. A purely statistical reason for this division is that whilst details are received of all injury accidents, there are only very limited data on damage only accidents. Personal injuries are divided into fatalities, serious injuries and slight injuries. Fatalities are recorded as such if death occurs within thirty days of the accident. A serious injury is defined as 'an injury for which the person is detained in hospital

---

[1] This chapter is contributed by permission of the Director, Transport and Road Research Laboratory. Crown Copyright 1973. Reproduced by permission of the Controller of HM Stationery Office.

as an in-patient, or any of the following injuries whether or not he is detained in hospital, fractures, concussion, internal injuries, crushings, severe cuts and lacerations, severe general shock requiring medical treatment [6]. This definition covers a much wider range of injury than the man in the street understands by serious—everything from a broken finger to incapacity for life.

Breakdown of costs

The costs involved in personal injury accidents can be divided into those that result from injuries to people and other costs, which will be mainly damage to vehicles and other property. The main costs relating to personal injury are medical treatment, ambulance costs, the loss of output whilst away from work and possibly after return to work, and the subjective costs. Some administrative costs are not easily divided between those attributable to injury and to damage, but overall these are not important items of cost and if necessary assumptions could be made which would be of the right order of magnitude.

The costs of human impairment can be divided into three categories:

(1) Those that result in a diversion of current resources. These are concerned with making good the results of the accident and are mainly medical costs.

(2) Loss of output (including unpaid output) which means that something which would have occurred in the future without the accident will not now occur. The loss of output due to injury does not raise any conceptual problems but in the case of those who are killed there is some dispute as to whether it should be taken net or gross of future consumption. The correct method depends on why the costs are needed. From a historical or ex post situation the net figure is the appropriate one, as that life is lost to the surviving community. From the ex ante situation or the position of the community that is planning action to prevent accidents, that is a community that includes those who will be killed if the accident occurs, then the gross loss is the correct figure. Loss of output is less certain when there is unemployment than in a full employment situation, which is the explicit or implicit assumption behind most of the calculations that have been made.

I.D.H.—4*

(3) Subjective or non-resource costs. These do not enter into any calculations of the National Income; none the less individually and collectively people are prepared to pay in order to avoid incurring them. Ways of measuring them are discussed in the next section.

Expenditures that lead to a diversion of current resources are mainly concerned with medical treatment; they may include costs of ambulances, of hospital in-patient treatment, of hospital out-patient treatment, general practitioners services, convalescence and nursing homes, home nursing for those with long-term incapacities, invalid cars and other equipment. Non-medical costs may be incurred by the police, the legal profession and insurance companies.

It is obvious that between individual accidents or casualties there is an enormous range. Even if only serious casualties are considered these could range from, say, £10 to £50,000.

The last year for which detailed calculations were made was 1963 [2] and estimates for later years are to some extent extrapolations of the 1963 data. The last years for which there is a published breakdown is 1968 [3]. In this year the total resource cost of accidents, that is excluding subjective costs, was £300m divided almost equally between personal injury and damage only accidents. The £155m resource cost of personal injury accidents is divided into

damage and administration	£56
loss of output	84
medical costs	15
	£155m

In addition the subjective costs were taken as £81m. Thus the costs of human impairment can be calculated to be £180m; the division between the different severities of casualty is given in Table 5.1.

The estimates that have been made at TRRL are based largely on a study of aggregate statistics and not on a detailed study of the actual costs of particular accidents. This procedure yields mean values but does not provide any estimate of the variation.

For example, hospital costs were estimated from information collected about the distribution of length of stay in hospital and number of out-patient visits of road accident cases and average costs per bed-day and per visit. (This would provide a distribution of hospital costs—with little detail at the top end of the distribution.) There is no way of combining this with information on the cost of damage on loss of output.

TABLE 5.1. **Analysis of costs of human impairment in road accidents (1968)**

Cost	Fatalities £m	Serious Injuries £m	Slight Injuries £m	All Injuries £m
Loss of output	67	16	1	84
Medical costs	*	11	3	14
Subjective	36	44	2	82
Total	103	71	6	180

* Less than £0·5m.

This method of assessment means that we are short of information about the most extreme serious casualties. For example, one of the surveys included someone who had already been over eight months in hospital but there was no means of estimating the probable length of stay or what medical costs would be incurred after discharge from hospital.

Subjective Costs

If it is decided that subjective costs should be included in the cost of accidents, the primary questions to be answered are: what are they, on what basis should they be measured, and what value should be placed on them?

What are subjective costs? Terms such as 'suffering' and 'bereavement' are usually used to explain the concept of subjective costs but if an attempt is to be made to value them then it is helpful to try to define them more precisely. The subjective costs of a death in a road accident can be divided according to who will suffer the cost:

(*a*) There is the cost to the person who is killed: principally the value to him of the remainder of his life. The community which is prepared to pay money to prevent accidents includes the persons who would be killed without these measures and it is therefore consistent to include the subjective values they place on saving their own lives. Other than for those killed instanteously, there is also the pain and suffering experienced by the casualty in the period between the accident and death.

(*b*) The mental anguish to the victims' relatives and friends. In some cases the net effect to some people will be a gain—distant relatives who leave legacies, deaths of those from whom one benefits indirectly by, for example, promotion. In the majority of cases there will be a net loss and the amount of the loss—although there are no sensible units in which to measure it—will depend on the spiritual and financial ties between the persons concerned and the length of time that the bereavement will take to heal. The length of time will depend partly on the ages of the deceased and of the bereaved.

(*c*) The shock to other persons directly and indirectly concerned in the accident.

(*d*) The loss to the community as a corporate body. In the case of road accidents where usually only one person and rarely more than a few persons are killed in any particular incident this will be small but it can be appreciable in the case of major disasters, e.g. the Chatham cadets.

The subjective costs of serious casualties may similarly be divided according to who experiences the cost:

(*a*) Costs to the casualty which may include: pain and suffering, inconvenience and worry—for example cancelling appointments and arranging for care of children—dullness of hospital or convalescence compared with normal life, and the permanent loss of some ability.

(*b*) Costs to relatives and friends may include: shock, the inconvenience of managing without the injured person, the inconvenience of managing for the injured and of visiting hospital, and possibly losses associated with some permanent disability to the injured.

(*c*) Costs to others involved in the accident and to those such as bystanders who become indirectly involved.

Slight casualties are of such a trivial nature that subjective costs will in most cases only amount to inconvenience: this however is still a cost. Similarly, although damage accidents by definition inflict no injury, they will always cause some inconvenience which in nearly all cases people would be willing to pay to avoid.

Possible bases for estimating subjective costs are:

(*a*) The amount that the casualty and others directly affected would be willing to pay, and be capable of paying, to avoid the accident.

(*b*) The amount that would exactly compensate the casualty and others directly or indirectly involved.

(*c*) The communities assessment.

The subjective cost of a death has been deduced from the calculation of the net loss of output which in the case of a death of a retired person or of one approaching retirement is negative, i.e. it is an economic gain. This can be thought of as the opportunity cost of keeping these people alive and is the minimum assessment of the value that the community places upon them. The premise being, that as the community is willing to keep its non productive members alive it values their lives at least at the amount which it would gain from their death. From the calculations based on age and sex groups the largest net loss was £5,000 [2] and this has been taken as the subjective cost of a death. This line of argument does not help to assess the average community valuation, nor how the valuation would vary with the age of the victim.

Valuation on own life

There are several possible ways in which the valuation which someone puts on his life could be assessed:

(i) His net worth plus the capitalized value of his possible future earnings less the capitalized cost of living at a subsistence level. This being the maximum amount he could pay.

(ii) The discounted value of his future consumption. This being taken as a measure of the enjoyment he would have received, it makes no allowance however for the enjoyment from things for which he would not have had to pay. There is no obvious way of placing a direct value on free goods such as the enjoyment of nature.

(iii) It has been suggested that the amount by which a man values his life can be determined by the amount for which he insures it but this assumes that he knows what the relevant probabilities are and he acts and can afford to act accordingly.

(iv) Jones-Lee [4] suggests that 'given certain assumption about human preferences, one can measure the money value which an individual places upon a given reduction of the probability of his own death by road accident'. He thinks that 'it may be possible to induce individuals to reveal their preferences in the comparatively abstracted context of a Von Newmann Morgenstern experiment'. He postulates that an individual can increase his income by working longer so in order to be able to pay more money so as to remain alive he can reduce his leisure time and/or his consumption. Whilst doubt can be thrown on many of his assumptions the major fallacy in his suggested method seems to be the assumption that people can appreciate changes in probability of the order of 0.00015.

In addition the subjective valuation of the deceased's relatives is also required. Conceptually this is harder to measure than the value which a man places on his own life—which is in some sense an absolute value. Any attempts to ask people soon after they were bereaved would almost certainly lead to over estimates.

For casualties, leaving aside those injuries which are so severe that the victim cannot be compensated, the choice is between what could be paid and what would compensate. In the less serious cases the two would be expected to coincide. If the aim is to place the assessment of accident costs on the same footing as time savings then the choice seems to be ability to pay. On grounds of equity, or from the point of view of the community, compensation seems to be the right criterion.

Ways of assessing the value that the community places on the saving of the life of one of its members include:

(a) Court cases; road accidents often result in cases being taken to court as a result of which awards are made to compensate for the damages that have been suffered. They are however of no use in assessing the subjective cost of a fatality. Court awards in the case of fatalities are almost entirely to cover objective costs and the maximum sum payable for loss of expectation of life is £400.

(*b*) A large number of organizations are concerned with spending money to save lives and a number of regulations make individuals spend money in order to reduce the risk of death or injury. For example, railways and airlines spend money to make travelling safer, money is spent on fire services and life boats, the medical authorities spend large amounts to save life both in the short term and, via research, in the long term. It seems unlikely that any of these outlays are based on an explicit valuation of a life to be saved but if the expenditures and the number of lives saved, or which it was expected to save, were known then implicit valuations could be calculated. If the implicit valuations by different organizations appeared to indicate a common value it could be argued that this was the amount that the community was willing to pay to save a life. Apart from collecting the data the major difficulty would be in determining what money was spent on saving life. For example, a large proportion of the effort of the fire services is directed to saving property and not life; and money spent on signalling by the railways increases the operating efficiency of the service as well as improving the safety.

It is necessary to distinguish between expenditure undertaken to prevent accidents and that undertaken after an accident has taken place in order to save a particular life or lives that were at risk; in such cases it is sometimes almost true that money is no object.

(*c*) Measures to prevent accidents are frequently only undertaken after there has been a public outcry as the result of an accident or accidents having taken place. Sometimes the outcry will be for road safety measures such as traffic lights or pedestrian bridges, sometimes for other measures such as filling in disused canals. An argument is that these are marginal measures that are undertaken at public request in order to save life and therefore the cost is an indication of the amount that the community places on the value of a life. The draw-back to the argument is that those who demand the measure, although they may be ultimately responsible for finding the money, or some of the money, probably do not take the cost very much into account whereas officials or councillors who supply the facility do not necessarily consider this the best way to spend money but do so partly as a result of public pressure. Frequently also there will be benefits other than the saving of life and costs other than the direct outlays.

(*d*) By considering the private costs of certain safety measures, such as seat belts, and the probabilities of these measures saving a life, it is possible to arrive at a lower limit value of life to those who adopt these measures. Conversely this gives the upper limit value to those who do not adopt the measures. The major defect in such an analysis is the underlying assumption that people are aware of the relevant probabilities.

The subjective valuation of casualties is in many ways easier than that of fatalities for although there is an enormous range of seriousness of casualties, the average costs are considerably lower and are conceptually more straight forward. A possible basis for valuing the subjective costs of a casualty is court awards. Court awards tend to be standardized for different categories of injury and these are listed in books of reference [*5; 9*]; for a given injury it is possible therefore to make a reasonable estimate of the damages that a court would award. There would be a problem in estimating an average value as little is known about the distribution of serious injuries by type of injury. A possible way of finding out this information would be to carry out a survey based on police records of those who had been seriously injured in a particular area in a particular period of time. The distribution by degree of severity is almost certainly very skew and a large sample would be required. An alternative method would be to obtain details directly from a hospital or hospitals about their serious road accident cases.

The subjective value of a serious injury was originally taken as £200 [*2*] and later as £500 [*3*]—the evidence for this figure is limited but an average for all serious injuries it is thought to be the right order of magnitude.

Ways of reducing impairment

The sum of human impairment resulting from road accidents may be reduced by a reduction in the number of accidents or by a reduction in the impairment that an accident causes. Measures may be primarily directed at reducing the number or the effect; frequently both will result. Sometimes the number might be reduced but the remaining or resulting accidents might be more severe. The accident rate per million vehicle miles travelled on motorways is much lower than on all-purpose roads (40 compared with 287 [*4*]), but the accidents that do occur are more serious

(0.1 deaths and, 0.5 serious injuries per injury accident on motorways compared with 0.03 and 0.3 on all purpose roads). Frequently actions taken to reduce the number of accidents will also result in the remaining accidents being less serious; for example the imposition of speed limits on the staggering of cross roads. Improvements to vehicle performance, such as better brakes are likely to reduce the number and the severity of accidents. Many of the measures that are aimed directly at reducing the human impairment that result from accidents—the use of seat belts for example—may not lead to any change in the number of accidents; unless, say, wearing a crash helmet leads to an undue feeling of security and the taking of more risks. On the other hand it is arguable that the taking of one security measure might make the wearer more accident conscious and lead to better driving.

Examples of costs of reducing impairment

Research into crash helmets for motor cyclists started at the Road Research Laboratory about twenty years ago. There have been two aspects of the work: studying the ways of improving the efficiency of helmets and estimating and then illustrating the value of wearing them. In 1967 Allsop [1] showed that if all motor cyclists and pillion passengers had worn helmets in 1964 there would have been 293 fewer fatalities, 946 fewer serious and 813 fewer slight injuries. This meant that the average yearly rate of return on the purchase of a helmet was about 150%. Looked at in another way, a helmet which cost on average from £2.50 to £3.00 would on average yield a benefit of nearly £4.00 per year. For moped riders the return would be smaller, about £0.50 per year: but even for them the helmet would pay for itself in five to six years.

Wilkins [10] used some of Allsop's data to assess the value of fitting anti-locking brakes on motor cycles. He concluded that there would be an economic gain provided the cost was below about £30 per machine.

A more complex situation which involves the comparison of different forms of impairment arises when considering whether to install crash barriers in the central reservations of motorways. Barriers are more likely to increase than decrease the total number of accidents but they will probably lead to a radical change in the type of accident. They will prevent a particularly dangerous and serious accident, head on collision between two vehicles travelling at high speed, but will lead to increased severity in other categories of accident. For example, with no barrier a vehicle might cross into the opposite carriageway and come to a stop without hitting anything but with a barrier installed it will hit the barrier and possibly bounce back onto the carriageway. Calculations by Moore and Jehu [8] in 1966 showed a low rate of return: accident savings of £460 per kilometre per year less £333 for maintenance costs from a capital cost of about £5,000. There are a number of reasons why this estimated return is rather low. Firstly Moore and Jehu used only the resource cost of accidents. If their calculation is repeated including the subjective costs given in LR 79 [2] then the annual return per kilometre is £590. Moreover the accidents that are saved by barriers tend to have a higher than average cost, largely because of the higher than average number of fatalities per fatal accident. If the calculations were reworked making an allowance for this and using the higher costs of a fatality given in LR 396 [3] the return would be quite high. On the other hand these estimates are based on data from the M1 where the traffic flow is higher than on other motorways.

References

1. Allsop, R. E., 'Costs and benefits arising if all motor cyclists wore safety helmets', *Ministry of Transport RRL Report LR 72*, Crowthorne, 1967 (Road Research Laboratory)

2. Dawson, R. F. F., 'Cost of road accidents in Great Britain', *Ministry of Transport RRL Report LR 79*, Crowthorne, 1967 (Road Research Laboratory)

3. Dawson, R. F. F., 'Current cost of road accidents in Great Britain', *Ministry of Transport RRL Report LR 396*, Crowthorne, 1971 (Road Research Laboratory)

4. Jones-Lee, M., 'Valuation of reduction in probability of death by road accident', *Journal of Transport Economics and Policy* III (1), 1969

5. Kemp, D. A. McL. and Kemp, M. S., *The Quantum of Damages*, London, Sweet and Maxwell, 1961

6. Ministry of Transport, *Road Accident Statistics*, Stats 20, London, HMSO, 1968

7. Ministry of Transport, Scottish Development Department and Welsh Office *Road Accidents 1968*, London, HMSO, 1969

8. Moore, R. L. and Jehu, V. J., 'Recent developments in barrier design', Ninth International Study Week in Traffic and Safety Engineering, Munich, 9–13 September 1968, Theme II *Traffic Engineering and Control*, 1968 *10*, (8)

9. Munkman, J., *Damages for Personal Injury and Death*, London, Butterworths, 1960

10. Wilkins, H. A., 'The cost and benefit of anti-locking brakes on motor cycles', *Ministry of Transport RRL Report LR 261*, Crowthorne, 1969 (Road Research Laboratory)

6 An Attempt to Assess the Cost of Home Care[1]

K. DUNNELL and *L. IDE*

Introduction

> What most disabled people want more than anything else is to lessen their dependence on other people, to get on with living their own lives as normally as they can in their own homes among their own family and wherever possible to have the opportunity of contributing to industry and society as fully as their abilities allow.

These words from Alfred Morris, putting forward the philosophy behind the 1970 Chronically Sick and Disabled Persons Bill, represent the feelings of the group of severely disabled patients whose cases have provided the material for this chapter.

In 1970 a case study was set up to investigate these patients who were under the care of the respiratory unit at St Thomas's Hospital, London. The 'responauts' all required regular mechanical respiratory support, following poliomyelitis, and in addition had varying degrees of residual paralysis which confined all of them to living in wheelchairs or beds. Their mobility varied from only being able to move the head, to being able to make partial use of arms and legs. Their respiratory impairment ranged from Grade II patients who regularly but not nightly, needed respiratory assistance during sleep but were able to breathe naturally during the day—to those Grade IV patients who need total artificial respiration at all times.

Because of their dependence on artificial respiration, all the responauts needed someone to be in constant attendance. Mainly for this reason, at the start of the study many patients were in hospital although some were managing to live at home with occasional in-patient stays. The main aim of the study was to discover what medical, technical, social and other support was

[1] This study was financed by the Department of Health and Social Security.

ideally required for responauts to live at home. In order to do this, a special panel was set up representing the research team, doctors from hospital and general practice, local authority health and social services and the Department of Health and Social Security.

The eighteen patients in the study were all assessed by the panel who then made recommendations about the optimum conditions for each patient. Where possible these were provided by statutory services, but supplemented by funds assigned to the experiment through the hospital. These were mostly used for the provision of resident nursing attendants. As a result fourteen responauts were living more or less securely in their own homes, three were settled in Cheshire homes and one in hospital.

We are reporting here on the attempt to measure the cost of caring for responauts at home and relating it to the cost of institutional care. The costs of home care are based on data collected for the fourteen patients living at home for a six-month period in 1972—January to June for eleven patients, July to December for two, and the three months July to September for one responaut. The hospital and Cheshire Home data are based on costs of the respiratory unit at the hospital and the two homes involved for the financial year 1971/72.

Problems

Only a small number of patients fulfilled the criteria for being in the study, i.e. they had paralysis and respiratory impairment resulting from poliomyelitis and were under the care of the respiratory unit. Even so, each one's needs were different because of variation in medical condition and economic and social circumstances. This meant that a case study approach was used which involved collecting detailed information from each responaut on all aspects of the costing exercise. In presenting results, difficulties arise in deciding how to group the responauts. For some items it is appropriate to group them by medical condition and for others by their family structure. For all items an average cost per responaut will be given.

As a group, patients in the study were not representative of permanently disabled people in society, nor of patients cared for by the respiratory unit. They were all middle class and most of them relatively well off. Only two of the responaut households had incomes under £30 per week, five had incomes of £60 or more. Needless to say their standard of living did not compare with the average for the whole country nor with that used by the Supplementary Benefits Commission. In order to measure the extra costs due to caring for a disabled person at home some kind of control group or other way of establishing a standard is ideally required for comparison. However, it was not felt that this was a practical possibility on a study of this kind.

Instead, the panel of experts set up for the study made decisions about the major items of expenditure for which responauts might have been expected to incur additional expense because of their medical condition. Items decided upon were: housing, home adaptations, equipment, nursing/attendant care, home help, medical and social services, fuel, light and power, telephone, laundry and transport. For some items, such as nursing/attendant care there was no problem about how much of it was due to disability because all of it was. But for others, such as heat, light and fuel and housing the amount of additional expenditure is more difficult to assess. The method we adopted for some items was to collect the actual expenditure on these items and compare them with that of households in the same income group in the Family Expenditure Survey.[1] We then assumed that the additional expense was due to the patients' medical condition. We also used built-in checks wherever possible. For example, the amount of electricity that respiratory machines used was measured and costed according to the amount of use.

Another problem encountered in the costing exercise arose from the idea of optimum conditions. When the panel decided on these for each patient they concentrated mainly on the need for nursing/attendants as the lack of these was the prime reason for patients having to return to hospital. Equipment needs were also fairly detailed. But it was in the area of housing, adaptations and transport that optimum conditions were not clearly defined. These are items which depend to an extent on the patient's expectations of quality of life, so realistically defined need was not possible. For example, many responauts had specially adapted ambulances to enable them to travel freely to friends, work, shopping, entertainment etc. Several of them had built sun lounges onto the back of their houses. Large items of expenditure

---

[1] Department of Employment, Family Expenditure Survey, Report for 1971, London, HMSO, 1972.

such as these aided the quality of life of responauts but it would be extending the concept of need to always label them necessities or as items principally acquired because of disability. On the other hand some patients were lacking in these areas. For example, a responaut may well be able to do a full time job, but because of lack of an ambulance and a driver to take him to and fro, this is an impossibility.

We collected data about what responaut's actually had, rather than what would have been most suitable for them or what they really needed. This means that sometimes in the costing we had to make subjective decisions to omit an item or to assign an extra cost for something the patient did not have but the panel considered necessary.

Much of the equipment, forms of transport and home adaptations patients had were purchased or paid for up to ten years before data was collected. In order to standardize these capital costs the replacement cost in 1971/72 was obtained. Middle range retail prices were used for current costs of items purchased by patients.

The cost of personnel for the home care of responauts

The main provision for the home care of responauts fell into three categories: nursing, attendance and domestic help. In practice in the costing it was not possible to separate the three functions. The specially employed responaut attendants were all trained to carry out some nursing duties—they also in some cases did domestic work and shopping etc. Some home helps employed by local authorities and privately employed cleaners performed an attendance function while doing housework. Relatives who cared for responauts frequently coped with all three aspects of care.

Table 6.1 shows the weekly average length of time that patients received different sorts of care. Nursing/attendance can be divided into three categories—that provided by paid staff, by relatives and voluntary workers[1] and the hours of the night when someone had to be on call.

This 'on call' time was also not paid for by anyone although often the person providing the service was an employed responaut attendant. However, as the average number of day time hours worked per week for those attendants was 56, it seems reasonable

---

[1] Only 9 hours for patient D was provided by a voluntary worker.

to assume that the 'on call' time is not rewarded financially,[1] like that of relatives. The nursing and domestic work in the next two columns of the table was all paid for, the services mostly being provided by local authorities although some was privately financed by the patients.

Table 6.2 is a summary of Table 6.1. Responauts have been grouped into four categories. As can be seen widowed or divorced women are most dependent on paid help and least dependent on unpaid help from relatives. This is because they do not live with relatives, having broken parental ties when marrying. They are also older than the single women in the next group therefore their mothers are either dead or very old. In contrast the four men living at home are more dependent than the other groups on

TABLE 6.1 **Average number of hours worked per week**

| | | Nursing attendance | | | | |
		Paid	Unpaid	On call at night	Nursing	Domestic
Widowed, divorced women	A	109	—	66	—	—
	F	128	—	63	<1	—
	D	84	9	56	1	—
Single women with mother	L	43	18	56	<1	—
	B	133*		56	—	—
	E	61	53	56	2	—
Married women	N	43**	35	60	3	**
	H	17	70	56	5	10
	O	57	5	56	7	6
	K	90	14	56	—	14
Men with resident woman	I	132	63	56	—	—
	C	53	71	56	2	5
	Q	—	112	56	4	—
	P	16	104	56	—	10

* Patient B's mother is employed as a responaut attendant.
** Attendance and domestic work is provided by a local authority home help.

---

[1] One responaut employed a night nurse for three nights a week.

unpaid help—in all cases provided by women—their mother, wife or co-habittee. As a consequence this group also receive fewer hours of care that is paid for. All groups require a similar provision of on call time.

TABLE 6.2   **Summary of nursing/attendance/domestic help received by responauts**

| | Nursing/attendance/domestic Number of hours per week | | |
	Paid	Unpaid	On call
3 widowed/divorced women	107	3	62
3 single women with mother	80	24	56
4 married women	63	31	57
4 men with resident woman	56	87	56
Average number of hours per week for 14 responauts	74	39	58

Having analysed the sort of care the responauts receive the next step is to cost it. The average hours worked each week total 171 —or three hours more than the hours in the week. Given that all the patients require virtually constant attendance it seems reasonable to assume that all this care is needed—therefore it should all be costed.

One approach is to cost the work that is paid for, i.e. that of responaut attendants, district nurses, home helps, private cleaners, nurses and housekeepers, etc. This theoretically is a straightforward procedure as the total costs of employing staff can be collected from their employers. One difficulty is that the specially employed attendants work an average 56 hour week but in fact are paid for 50 hours work.

In this case the imaginary cost of these six overtime hours per week can be added.

The major problem of course is what to do about the time that nobody pays for. Do we assume that care provided by wives, mothers and retired husbands is freely (in the economic sense) available as society as a whole thinks it is, or do we assign a cost to it? The latter could be done in two ways. Firstly by saying that if these women (they all are women except one) went out to work instead, they would earn the average women's weekly wage in that 39 hours. Alternatively, one could use the cost of employing an attendant for 39 hours a week. Both these costs will be similar, so the decision really is whether to cost it or not.

The same sort of problem arises with the 'on call' time. It may be fair to assume that where a relative who would normally be living with the patient provides on call care it need not be costed. That provided by specially employed attendants could be costed at on call nursing rates. The first assumption would seem reasonable if the same relatives were paid (or costed) for their day time work. Table 6.3 shows how the caring time in Table 6.2 can be costed in this way.

TABLE 6.3   **The costs, both real and imaginery, of personnel to care for the fourteen responauts at home for a week**

		£	p
Paid care—1,036 hours			
Responauts' attendants	923 hours at average 49p	452	27
Home help and cleaning	88 hours at 49p	43	12
District nursing 31·5 visits at 93p = 22 hours		29	30
Private nursing 3 hours at £1		3	00
		£527	69
Unpaid care—546 hours			
Assign a cost of 50p per hour		273	00
On call time—812 hours			
Provided by paid attendants	328 hours at 30p	98	40
Provided free by resident relatives	484	00	00
Total weekly cost of 14 responauts' care		£899	09

Average weekly cost per patient = £64.22

Other personnel who visited patients in their homes were general practitioners and social workers. The responauts received an average of 7 home visits per year from general practitioners and 2 from social workers. These visits represent four hours per year of a doctor's time per patient and four and a half social worker hours (both include travelling time).

The mechanical equipment that patients require at home needs regular maintenance. This is mainly carried out by engineers employed by the hospital. As patients live scattered over South-East England the travelling involved is fairly substantial. Patients have an average of seventeen maintenance visits per year or an average of 49 engineer hours, 29 of which are travel time. It would be possible to assign a cost per patient for this machine maintenance. However, the cost of employing engineers, providing transport and spare parts etc. is included in the hospital costing as the same personnel maintain hospital equipment. Assigning a cost per hour and a cost per mile travelled it is estimated that maintenance of responaut equipment costs in the region of £60 per patient per year. Those responauts with severe respiratory impairment (Grade IV) have three times as much machine maintenance as the other responauts.

The personnel discussed in this section were mainly provided by the health and social services who therefore bear the costs. The next group of items to consider are the on going costs to patients of living at home.

Current direct costs

(1) Medical

As expected, most of the medical necessities of these patients were supplied through the National Health Service. As they would have been needed whether or not the patient was cared for at home or in hospital there was no need to compare the absolute cost. However, patients did incur small costs, mainly because of their equipment. They needed to purchase, for example, covers for wheelchairs, bed linen and foam rubber cushions and pads. All these items needed replacing fairly frequently and responauts spent an average of nine pounds a year on them.

It has been possible to compare three of these items of expenditure with the Family Expenditure Survey results: fuel, light and power, telephone and laundry.

(2) Fuel, light and power

Detailed information was collected from the responauts about their expenditure on gas, electricity, fuel oil and solid fuel. Most patients were able to give us the costs for a full year, the others for two or three-quarters. The expenditure for a half year, covering a winter and summer quarter, was calculated for eleven responaut households. (We have not been able to obtain information from two households—we cannot use that from a third because they feel unable to disclose their income.) This expenditure was compared with that of households in the same income group in the FES. All responauts spent more on fuel, light and power than the expected amount. The average additional expenditure over the six-month period was £43.29. All patients received rebates from hospitals to cover the cost of running their machines—an average of £9.48 per half year. Thus the average net extra expenditure by responauts was £33.80 or £1.30 a week. This sum can be interpreted as representing the extra cost due to disability incurred most probably because households had to be heated all day and responauts often needed to be kept warmer than the average person.

The real cost of caring for patients at home would be greater—it would be the marginal cost of the additional adult living in the house plus the sum due to disability. One way of measuring this would have been possible if we had information about expenditure before patients were discharged home. Another way would be to compare expenditure of say three and four adult households in the same income group. Neither of these were in fact possible because the data were not available.

(3) *Telephone*
The calculation of extra expenditure on the telephone was more complicated because only 38% of households in the FES have telephones. This proportion varies from 13% of households with incomes under £10 a week to 85% of those with incomes over £80. The problem was overcome by making the assumption that because all the responauts had telephones and because local authorities are now empowered to provide telephones for the disabled,[1] it was reasonable to compare expenditure of responauts with the FES expenditure figures recalculated to provide a figure for telephone subscribers only.

---

[1] Chronically Sick and Disabled Persons Act 1970, Chapter 44 section 2(1) h.

The average expenditure of the responauts on the telephone was £28.81 per half year. The expected expenditure was £16.31, therefore the extra was £12.50 per half year. Five patients had the rental paid for them (£10.00 per half year) by either the local authority or a charity. All the additional expenditure by responauts must be on calls. How much of the expenditure on calls (as opposed to rental) can be seen as a need, the cost of whose provision we should include in this exercise, is open to question. However, as the telephone is probably the most important medium for communication for responauts, given that their mobility and writing capabilities are severely limited, it seems reasonable to count it all.

(4) Laundry

Responaut households spent an average £18.00 per year on laundry. Comparable households in the FES would have spent only £3.31 per year. This represents an extra £14.69 a year which on our assumption was due to the medical condition of the patient—many of them spent much longer than the average in bed, more towels and linen are required for washing and nursing.

(5) Housing

The basic prerequisite of discharging a disabled patient from hospital, is that he or she has a home to go to. Of the fourteen responauts now at home, eleven had homes to which they could return, either their own family homes or parental homes. It seems therefore that for these eleven the capital cost of providing housing in the community need not be considered. The other three responauts did not have homes to be discharged to. They have found rented accommodation, one a ground floor local authority flat, one a privately rented house, the third has become a member of a family and pays board and lodging. The capital cost of these homes could be derived by using for example the cost to the local authority of building a three-bedroomed ground floor flat for a disabled person. Other capital costs involved in housing are those for adaptations to the houses to make them suitable for disabled people. Twelve responaut homes needed adapting in some way or other. Some common types of alterations and provisions were french windows, ramps, pathways, door widening and the removal of awkward corners. These are the kinds of items that local authorities are generally willing to finance. The average sum spent on the fourteen homes was £310.29.

In addition, five responauts had privately (or in one case a charity had) provided sun lounges, garages or extra rooms. The responauts all reported that these additions had been made because of their disability but as it is questionable whether or not they should reasonably be included on the grounds of need we have costed them separately. The average cost to the fourteen patients was £220.43 bringing the average total cost of adaptations to £530.72.

The next items to consider are the running costs of the homes. Again for those homes which already existed, rent, mortgage repayments and rates will not be affected by the household being rejoined by a disabled person. The three responauts who had to find themselves homes on discharge from hospital paid an average of £337.55 per year for rent, rates and home insurances. One would expect, however, that expenditure on maintenance and repairs of houses would be an additional expense for all responaut houses. Not only were they less able than most people to carry out this work themselves but wheelchairs, other equipment and the considerable nursing work that was carried out created an above average amount of wear and tear. On average the households spent £31.96 per year more on maintenance and repairs than would have been expected using FES figures.

Table 6.4 summarizes the annual direct costs to responauts and health and welfare services which appeared to arise because of their disability. Responaut households had an additional expenditure of £128.25 a year on medical needs, fuel light and power, telephone, laundry and house maintenance. Hospitals, local authorities and/or charities spent another £38.96 on electricity rebates and telephone rental.

(6) *Transport*
Eleven of the fourteen responauts living at home owned specially adapted motor vehicles. We collected information about the length of all journeys responauts made in these. The maintenance costs of the vehicles, the miles per gallon and the cost of journeys made by responauts without private transport were also obtained for the six-month period. Two responauts also had to employ drivers on a regular basis to drive them to work. Maintenance of vehicles was a large item of expenditure for responauts, often

TABLE 6.4   **Some extra annual costs attributable to disability**

Item	Expense for		Total Expenditure
	Patient	Health or Social Services	
Linen, foam, etc.	£9.00		£9.00
Fuel, light, power	67.60	£18.96	86.56
Telephone	5.00	20.00	25.00
Laundry	14.69		14.69
House maintenance	31.96		31.96
Total	£128.25	£38.96	£167.21

because their vans were old. The annual average cost of maintenance and repairs was £124.90. The running cost of vehicles, that is petrol and drivers pay, and the cost of taxis for one responaut without transport, averaged £49.78 per patient per year. Thus total average expenditure on transport for each responaut was £174.68 per annum.

The ownership of a specially adapted vehicle adds greatly to the quality of life of responauts. It enables them to travel to see friends, relatives and places other than the homes in which they live. For the two single women in the study it allowed them to earn a living. However, it may be argued that it is stretching the concept of need to include the cost of individual transport for leisure in the cost of community care.

It would seem appropriate though, to include the cost of transport which disabled people use in order to go out to work. Because both patients in the study who worked outside the home had to hire drivers, the average cost of their transport is high—£396.25 per year. This is probably a realistic cost—as somebody always has to spend time driving the responaut wherever he goes.

(7) *Equipment*
Lists were designed, with the help of medical and nursing staff

in the respiratory unit, of all possible equipment that responauts might have. Information on type of equipment, as well as date of supply and supplier and cost, was obtained from each patient on a home visit. As a result we have information about all the equipment that patients had. However, much of this was needed whether or not the patient was being cared for at home. All that concerns us here are the extra capital costs incurred because of discharge from hospital. Extra capital equipment has been defined as those additional items which a patient needed to live at home, which would not have been provided as extras, if the patients were in hospital, e.g. bell systems, heaters, trolleys, electric wheelchairs and some respiratory equipment. This implied the exclusion of most respiratory equipment for each patient, except where respirators were provided, as part of a wheelchair to enable greater mobility at home, e.g. Cavendish chair, as spares for emergencies and to go on holiday. The costing does not include provision of emergency generators for power failure, as most patients are currently either admitted to hospital or lent generators by the GPO. However, consideration is being given to the provision for each patient of a generator in the future.

Table 6.5 shows the capital cost of providing this extra equipment for groups of responauts with differing degrees of respiratory impairment. The first row deals with what we call medical equipment, that is, hoists, wheelchairs with built-in respirators,

TABLE 6.5   **Average capital expenditure on extra equipment for each respiratory impairment grade (£)**

Respiratory Impairment	Grade II	Grade III	Grade IV	All Patients
Medical Equipment e.g. hoists, wheelchairs, spare respirators	£955	£239	£1,386	£811
Non-Medical Equipment e.g. Possum, installation of telephones, heaters	£126	£329	£700	£381
Total average cost	£1,081	£568	£2086	£1,192

spare respirators, electric wheelchairs, accessories for these machines and other equipment like bedpans and foam padding. As can be seen, the cost of the extra medical equipment to live at home is not related to degree of respiratory impairment. Grade III patients require much less *extra* equipment because what they need in hospital is adequate at home. Grade II patients require much more portable equipment and Grade IV patients need special respirator chairs as well as emergency equipment because of their total dependency. The next row deals with extra non-medical equipment, for example, Possums, telephones, typewriters, heaters, reading stands and trolleys. The expenditure on these is related to degree of impairment. The greater the disability the more the need for electrical aids.

(8) *The cost of hospital care*

The basic cost of hospital care falls on the health service. The problem in this costing exercise is to find an appropriate cost with which to compare the home care costs. We have collected information on the revenue expenditure of the respiratory unit from which responauts were discharged and which is still responsible for their care. The sum spent on medical and surgical appliances has been subtracted from the total expenditure because it represents the equipment that responauts used whether they were in or out of hospital plus those pieces of equipment which we have costed separately in the preceding section.

In 1971/2 the calculated cost of an in-patient week was £229. In 1970/1 it was £131. This large increase is mainly accounted for by the changing nature of the unit's workload following the discharge of many longstay patients like the responauts in this study. The unit now tends to care for more patients and copes with more admissions and discharges but the number of occupied bed days per year has fallen. This makes the cost of an in-patient week higher. A more realistic cost for comparison for 1971/2 may be to take the 1970/1 cost and increase it by 10% giving a cost per in-patient week of £144. A similar figure is arrived at by taking total revenue expenditure for 1971/2 and dividing it by the number of in-patient weeks in 1970/1.

Other costs were incurred by patients and their families, for example the cost of employing a housekeeper or child minder to replace a hospitalized mother, loss of the disabled person's earnings because of hospitalization and the cost of visiting the patient in hospital. Because we have not been able to carry out a before-and-after study on these cases, and only one patient was still living in hospital, we have not been able to measure these costs. However, it should be noted that ideally costs such as these should be included.

Cheshire homes

Three responauts lived in Cheshire Homes. The actual cost of keeping a patient in the two Cheshire Homes involved in the study was obtained from the Treasurers. The costs were the average cost per resident week—it was not possible to identify the costs of an individual patient. The actual cost of looking after a disabled person in a Cheshire home is greater than the cost to the Local Authority or Hospital which pays; because about a fifth of the total expenditure is financed from charitable sources or by efforts of the homes themselves. The average actual weekly cost of the care of the three responauts was £33.00. In addition each resident received an average three hours a week of regular voluntary help which, if costed at 50p an hour, raises the cost to £34.50.

The cost is considerably less than that of hospital care. Cheshire homes do not have the enormous overhead costs of a London Teaching Hospital, neither do they employ expensive medical staff. Only people requiring minimum amounts of nursing care are suitable for residence in a Cheshire home. The three responauts were all in the least disabled grade of respiratory impairment.

Summary and conclusion

Before summarizing our conclusions, we should point out two of the limiting factors within which we conducted our study: we restricted our costing to items which disabled people can clearly be seen to need and spend money on. Furthermore, we did not try to measure the cost to the family, if there is one, of the stress of caring for such a patient and the loss of leisure time and freedom entailed.

The provision of personnel to nurse and perform domestic and attendance duties was the biggest cost item. Less than half the care received by patients was actually paid for. The rest was provided free by relatives and resident attendants (who were paid for day time work). When all this care, except night time on call by resident relatives, was costed the weekly figure per patient was £64.22. This is probably unrealistically low because of the lack of staff who are prepared to work for rates of pay of 50p per hour. The weekly costs of other manpower like general practitioners, social workers, maintenance engineers and rebates for electricity and telephone average an additional £2.26. Capital expenditure on adaptations amounted to an average £530.72.

Expenses that the patients themselves incurred for extra fuel, light, power, telephone, laundry, linen and house maintenance were on average £2.46 a week. For this particular group of patients the cost of housing was not an important item because in most cases suitable housing already existed. However, this was a very unusual situation for not only were there homes to go to, but they were big enough to accommodate the necessary resident attendants. A more realistic costing would be the capital needed to provide the accommodation and the average £6.49 per week cost of housing to the three responauts who had to find homes to rent on discharge from hospital.

Three categories of patients stand out from these fourteen cases as being particularly costly to care for in the community. The first is the widowed, divorced or single middle-aged woman who has no family. This group's dependence on specially employed care is not only more expensive but their position in the community is more precarious because of this dependence. Resident attendants are very difficult to recruit and tend to be foreign girls who only stay for short periods of time. A breakdown in provision of attendants usually means a return to hospital for social reasons. The second group is made up of those patients who no longer have a home in which they and the people who care for them can go and live. Again the problem is not just an economic one—but the supply of suitable housing is very short.

The third category of responauts are those who are able to find employment outside their homes. They have a real need for specially adapted transport and a driver. Our costing of travel has shown that these patients spend in the region of a third of their earnings on this, even taking into account their exemption from road tax.

An important consideration in making a comparison between home and hospital care for these patients is to what extent resources can be diverted from the hospital to the community.

At the present time this is difficult but the reorganized and hopefully unified health service which came into being in 1974 may make this process easier. In theory it might seem that the discharge of this group of responauts—some of them almost permanent patients—would have resulted in greatly lowering the cost of the respiratory unit. As we have seen this did not happen. Two factors are important here. Firstly the responauts are dependent on the hospital for specialist care, for periodical admission for surveillance and for emergency admission in medical or social crises. Thus the unit has to remain in existence.

The second factor is that gradually, with the discharge of long-term patients, the nature of the unit's work has changed. In the four years 1969–72 the number of admissions per year doubled from 39 to 85, average length of stay fell from 67 to 20 days and a third more patients were cared for—51 compared to 30. Although the unit has decreased the number of bed occupancy days, the throughput of patients is greater and more acute care is being given.

So far we have talked only of costs—but of course one of the main purposes of the study was to benefit the patient. All the responauts involved in this case study are intelligent, highly motivated people who faced spending the rest of their lives in hospital. Their aim has been to live more independently out of hospital. These sorts of benefits to patients and their families are not as yet measurable in money terms. But there is little doubt in the minds of the patients, those caring for them and involved in the study, that those responauts who have succeeded in living out of hospital have benefited in terms of independence, happiness and the whole quality of life outside an institution. These factors are particularly important to consider in relation to the permanently disabled, for the choice is between the provision of as normal a life as possible at home—or institutionalization and dependence for the rest of the person's life.

7 The Cost of Community Care and the Burden on the Family of Treating the Mentally ill at Home

P. SAINSBURY and J. GRAD DE ALARCON

The study we want to describe deals with the 'cost' of one of the most common causes of prolonged impairment—mental disorder; but our observations will for the most part be limited to one facet of the problem: the cost to the family or household of caring for a mentally ill member. Our reasons for doing this and the currency in which cost is measured will, we hope, become clearer if we first outline the background to the project and its objectives.

The introduction of the NHS not only raised the standards in our mental hospitals but also improved the quality of extramural psychiatric services; an important feature of the services was that they were becoming increasingly community orientated. Then in 1959 the Mental Health Act dismantled the remaining barriers between the mental hospital and the community it served; and the promotion of 'community care' became the declared policy of the Ministry of Health. But this course was advocated before any systematic evaluative research into the effects of such a policy had been undertaken.

It was not the Ministry that first attempted to do this, but (*pace* Rothschild) the MRC's Clinical Psychiatry Unit. The need for research into services is now, of course, amply recognized by the DHSS. Nevertheless its present policy of replacing mental hospitals by psychiatric beds in district hospitals supported by community services is a further extension of a trend. The cost of this trend remains largely un-assessed in terms of the patient's suffering, in the quality of his daily life—especially if he is chronically handicapped—and in the burden it imposes on the community. The problem to which we mainly addressed our efforts, therefore, was whether community centred services can alleviate the social and clinical impairment of the mentally ill without increasing the burden on the community, which for all practical purposes means the members of the patient's family. But we were also interested in other questions germane to the cost of human impairment. Whether, for example, a community service deployed its personnel and material resources more efficiently than a more traditional hospital-centred one such that needs were being met more effectively, or whether a comparable degree of clinical improvement was being achieved by fewer contacts with the hospital and its personnel.

The current enthusiasm for the extramural care of the mentally ill was pre-empted by Dr Carse at Graylingwell Hospital; he introduced a community psychiatric service in Worthing in 1957, and this was extended to Chichester and district a year later. His purpose was strictly practical; to reduce admissions to a mental hospital which had become overcrowded. It was only after we began the evaluation, that other reasons for promoting this form of care were advocated; the revised tenet of the service being that treatment given in the patient's usual family and social setting is more beneficial than when given in an institution. So the initially rather ill-defined objectives were later reformulated as follows: to reduce the hospital's admission rate; to facilitate discharge and thereby reduce institutionalization; and to explore alternatives to admission for the increasing numbers of geriatric patients.

To achieve these ends new provisions for extramural treatment were introduced. Firstly, a day hospital, the administrative centre for the service, was opened; out-patients sessions were increased, and a decision was taken to treat certain patients in their homes. Secondly, every new referral to the service was first examined, either at home, or at the day centre or at an out-patient clinic, before the decision whether to admit the patient or to give treatment extramurally was taken.

Another feature of this service was close collaboration with the general practitioners rather than with the local authority social services; its emphasis was therefore on clinical rather than social care—a kind of GP psychiatry in which the consultant visits the home and makes his own assessment of the family's circumstances and needs.

The evaluation

The design was to compare all referrals to the community service in Chichester (population 120,000) with those to the more conservative hospital-centred service in Salisbury (population 116,000). As only 14% of referrals were admitted to the mental hospital in Chichester whereas 52% were in Salisbury, the Chichester service could be fairly designated as community based. Though the clinicians collaborated closely in the organization of the project, the research team remained independent.

The research aims

As the objectives of the new service had only been loosely formulated, deciding on the principal aims of the evaluation was not easy; but what then seemed relevant to the problems of a community care service, and what was feasible from the standpoint of method and resources, led us to the following priorities:

What are the effects of introducing a community service on:

(1) Who gets referred? that is how are the referral rates of different social and clinical categories of patients affected. Whether or not more people are seen, and whether they are seen earlier in their illness are questions relevant to cost and impairment.

(2) Who gets admitted and who treated in the community? Duration of stay, case of discharge, and hence the extent to which patients are exposed to the risk of becoming institutionalized, are also matters that relate closely to problems of impairment in the psychiatric patient.

(3) The patients' clinical and social outcome? Again if this is better than expected, then both impairment and cost might be less.

(4) The patient's family and the extent to which his household is burdened? At that time the consequences to the community (and patients' families are those most immediately affected) of caring for the mentally ill patients outside hospital who would previously have been admitted, had not been considered; though Tizard and Grad had reported adverse effects on families having a subnormal child living at home [2]. So the possibility that the social cost to families might be considerable was very real.

Originally, we had planned a comparison of the economic costs of the hospital and community services, but the practical difficulties proved too great. Nevertheless we were able to compare the two services on the number of days each patient spent in hospital and of contacts made with the services during two years. May [3], however, successfully costed five methods of treating schizophrenic patients in hospital and was able to show that drug treatment was not only more effective than psychotherapy but also that it was less expensive.

Methods

The plan of the study was to compare the social and clinical characteristics of all patients referred during eighteen months to the community service (Chichester and district) with similar data on all referrals to the hospital-based service in Salisbury and district (the control). The two census districts were demographically and geographically similar except for a higher proportion of elderly on the Sussex coast, and the material resources and health personnel available was alike in each, though Salisbury had more social workers. As there were no private psychiatrists in either district, the referral rates specific for the different demographic categories could be compared.

In order to compare the two services on factors determining admission and extramural care, the patient's outcome, and the effects on their families, the homes of a one in three sample were visited in each district soon after they had seen the psychiatrist and again two years later. The responsible relative was interviewed and the appropriate questionnaires and rating scales completed.

To obtain the *epidemiological* data a Cumulative Case Register was set up in each district. In this way, some 80 items of social and clinical information were systematically recorded on all new referrals to the two services. The data was collected by the service psychiatrists, every one of whom filled up the research team's itemized record form which they used instead of the hospital case sheets. A reliability study [1] in which the first 90 referrals were independently interviewed by two psychiatrists showed a satisfactory level of agreement on the principal items of clinical history, symptoms and broad diagnostic categories.

To obtain details of the patients' social and family characteristics, the research psychiatric social workers visited the homes of the 1 in 3 sample and completed a schedule in the course of a semi-structured interview with the responsible relative. Two visits were made: one a month after referral and the other two years later. On both occasions the burden on each family was measured in four ways. First by rating the effect the patient had on the work, leisure, income and health of the family; on the children and on relationships with neighbours; and the amount and type of care the household had to provide. Each item was rated as 'none', 'some' or 'severe'. Secondly, an *overall* rating of burden on the basis of all the information available was made at the end of the visit. Thirdly, a family *problem score* was derived from the separate ratings. And finally, we listed, in laymen's terms, the kinds of behaviour most likely to worry the informants; and they rated these. In addition, the social and welfare needs of the family were estimated at the first visit, and then the work actually done during the two years was recorded; similarly all domicillary out-patient and day hospital contacts with the service and days in hospital were registered.

The extent to which families were affected was assessed on the one hand from their burden ratings and scores when the patient was first referred and two years later, and on the other by comparing the changes in these scores in the two services, a measure we designated *relief of burden*.

Relief of burden was also used to measure outcome. The other outcome assessments were: ratings of clinical improvement made by the psychiatrist treating the patient when he discharged him; ratings of mental state made by the research psychiatrist at two years; and ratings of improvement made by the responsible relative, the family doctor and by the patient, also at two years.

We therefore attempted to look at the cost of mental illness from two principal viewpoints: (1) By comparing the effect of services on patients to see in whom hospital and in whom extramural care had adverse consequences—the price the patient pays for community or institutional care; (2) by assessing the cost to their families of the vaunted community psychiatry.

The *severity of illness* of patients referred in Chichester and Salisbury were very similar when assessed by diagnosis and by incidence of symptoms; but they were also closely matched on the number of problems they had caused their families when first seen. The extent to which their behaviour was disturbing to others provided an independent measure of severity (see Table 7.1).

The numbers referred and visited, and the populations at risk are shown in Table 7.2.

TABLE 7.1   **Effects on families when the patients were first referred**

	Chichester (N:271)	Salisbury (N:139)
Problem Scores	%	%
0–1	38	32
2–3	25	24
4–5	14	15
6+	23	29
Burden Ratings	%	%
None	40	29
Some	42	46
Severe	18	25

TABLE 7.2   **Numbers referred and referral rates to the two services**

	Chichester	Salisbury
Patients referred in experimental period	823	585
Sample for follow-up study	271	139
Cohort surviving after 2 years	223	120
Annual referral rate per 1,000 aged 15+	6·8	5·3
Annual admission rate per 1,000 aged 15+	1·0	2·8
Populations		
Male aged 15–64	34,070	34,470
Female aged 15–64	39,080	37,230
Male aged 65+	8,040	6,690
Female aged 65+	13,320	9,660

Who gets referred

The Community Service was more efficiently meeting the needs of the mentally ill because for nearly all social and clinical categories of patients the referral rates were higher in the Chichester than in the Salisbury district: the community-care referral rates, specific for age, sex, civil status, class and mode of living, were *significantly* higher for the elderly, single, the poor, old men living alone—that is those groups which had previously tended to suffer neglect. Of greater importance was that those with *the more serious* forms of mental disorder were preferentially referred in Chichester. So extending services to the community can reduce the likelihood of mental impairment not only by offering care to more people, but by also providing it for those whose needs are greatest.

Another finding clearly distinguished the relative costs of the two forms of care. When the referral rates by duration of illness were compared, the community service patients were being seen earlier. The proportion who had been ill for six months or less being 57% in Chichester and 45% in Salisbury. Forty per cent of the Salisbury patients had been ill for over two years before seeing a psychiatrist; a surprisingly long period of hardship for so many to endure before getting help.

Admission and cost

Following referral to the psychiatrist three times as many patients were admitted in the hospital-centred service as compared with the community one; and throughout the follow-up period one-and-a-half as many were admitted. Moreover, those who were admitted in the community service, (*a*) had a mean duration of stay in hospital during the two years which was significantly shorter than in the control, (*b*) were re-admitted about twice as often, and (*c*) fewer patients were still in hospital at the end of the two years though the difference was quite small. Nevertheless, taking these three findings together the risk of suffering the common secondary impairment of a prolonged stay in a mental hospital, namely institutionalization, is probably less in the community service, not only because it admits fewer patients but because it is equally prepared to discharge them.

Social rather than clinical factors were determining admission in Chichester as compared with Salisbury. Thus, such adverse social and family circumstances as low social class or high family problem scores were more closely related to admission in the community service than in the 'control' one; but these factors can delay discharge too. Unless the family's circumstances are rigorously assessed and appropriate welfare action taken to make discharge possible, the selected groups of patients who get admitted under this policy are in danger of getting trapped in hospital and of suffering both social and clinical deterioration.

Outcome

The next problem we looked at was how the introduction of a community service affects the course and outcome of the patient's illness. Do patients treated in the community suffer less impairment and, if so, what kinds of patient are likely to benefit.

Taking the most extreme measure of injurious consequences first, we found the mortality rates were identical in the two services. Nevertheless, a widely held misgiving about community care is that the mentally ill patient living at home is more exposed to the risk of suicide than is his more closely supervized counterpart in hospital. Walk [4] tested this view by examining the incidence of suicide among all patients within a year of contact with the service for the five-year periods preceding and following its introduction. He found the suicide rate of the elderly, the group for whom the new service appeared to have provided most support, had decreased significantly in the second period. The work of Barraclough and others [5] also suggests that an improvement in the standards of extramural psychiatric services, such as more efficient follow up facilities and management of the psychiatric patient by general practitioners, might very probably prevent a proportion of suicides—an intolerable charge for inadequate services.

The outcome ratings of the treating psychiatrists, of the research psychiatrists and the patients' own assessment were quite highly inter-correlated; they agreed that outcome was better in the hospital service; though when assessed on the remission of presenting symptoms Chichester was superior, at least as regards the most treatable of disorders—the depressive illnesses.

The family doctors and the responsible relatives ratings correlated closely but showed less agreement with psychiatric opinions: the consensus was that outcome in the two services did not differ. It was of interest that those whose appraisal was probably based on overall social behaviour should conflict with the more clinically weighted views of the psychiatrists. Another, but independent measure of outcome and of the comparative cost in social terms of the two services was the relief each gave to *severely* burdened families after 2 years. This did not show any difference between them (see table 7.3 below). Thus, the view of the patients and psychiatrists was that Chichester community service was clinically less effective than the control; but the patients' families did not agree with this. The likely reasons for the community service's shortcomings will be more apparent when the effects on the family are described.

TABLE 7.3   **Percentage of families relieved of burden after month and two years later**

	% Relieved			
	At one month		At two years	
	Chichester	Salisbury	Chichester	Salisbury
Some burden at referral	24	36	59	86
Severe burden at referral	62	61	66	68
Any burden at referral	35	44	60	82

The cost to the family

1. Before referral

When the patients were first referred for psychiatric treatment the burden on their families was the same in the two districts. In both areas about two-thirds of the families were suffering some hardship, and in one-fifth it was severe (see table 7.1). In order therefore to get a general estimate of the effect of the untreated patients on their households the two samples were added together and the extent of different types of problems examined.

More than half our informants felt excessive anxiety due, they said, to worrying about the patient (see table 7.4). A fifth of them attributed neurotic symptoms (insomnia, headaches, excessive irritability, and depression) to their concern about the patient's behaviour. The social and leisure activities of a third of the families had been restricted; nearly a third had had their domestic routine upset (housework, shopping, and so on); about a quarter had had their income reduced by at least 10%, and a tenth by more than half. In a quarter of the families someone had to stay away from work. In more than a third, the children were disturbed. Further, in 30% of families the patient needed nursing care or supervision at home, of whom a half needed constant attention so that the patient could hardly ever be left alone [8].

TABLE 7.4 **Family problems**

| Effect on | % Families | | |
	Some Disturbance	Severe Disturbance	Total Burden
Health of closest relatives			
Mental	40	20	60
Physical	28	—	28
Social and leisure activities of			
family	14	21	35
Children	24	10	34
Domestic routine	13	16	29
Income of family	14	9	23
Employment of others than the			
patient	17	6	23

Considering the rather conservative nature of our measures, these figures reveal the exorbitant amount of social hardship that mental illness inflicts, and encouraged us to think that a measure of its reduction would be one way of assessing the effectiveness of psychiatric care. And when the further fact that 60% of families had already suffered these hardships for more than 2 years is taken into account, then the full cost of domiciliary care is sufficiently serious to place the onus of proof on those who advocate the benefits of extramural treatment.

In order also to define the families' problems in clinical terms we asked them to tell us which aspects of the patient's behaviour had been worrying. Most troublesome was the constant harping on bodily complaints (see table 7.5). Next were their fears that the patient might harm himself. But dangerous and socially embarrassing behaviour, and behaviour conspicuous enough to provoke comment from neighbours were the three items least frequently reported.

The amount and severity of the load the family carries will depend, among other things, on the characteristics of the patient. Burden was not related to the sex of the patient, but it did increase with age. Forty per cent of patients over 65 were rated as being a severe burden at referral compared with 11% of those below 40 years. And when the effects on the family were related to *psychiatric diagnosis*, families most adversely affected were those in which the patient was suffering from an organic psychosis or from a personality disorder. The young neurotic and depressed patients were causing least trouble (nevertheless because they were less conspicuous they later became a source of concern, see below). The *psychiatric symptoms* that related significantly to causing a severe burden were: aggression, delusions, confusion and inability to care for self. Although somatic complaints were most often reported by relatives as causing them concern, it was the demented, bed-fast patient needing constant attention who interfered drastically with home life. The other clinical feature strongly associated with severity of burden was duration of the patient's illness.

TABLE 7.5   **Patient's behaviour described by family as worrying.**

Behaviour	% Families (410 patients)
Frequent complaints about bodily symptoms	38
A danger to himself (suicide or accident)	34
Importunate and demanding	34
Behaving oddly or expressing peculiar ideas	27
Unco-operative and contrary	26
Constantly restless or over-talkative by day	23
Troublesome at night	21
Threatening the safety of others	12
Objectionable, rude, or embarrassing	8
Causing trouble with neighbours	7

2. Amount of family burden during two years

Three hundred and twenty-nine patients out of the 410 were alive two years later. In this cohort that survived there was a trend for all aspects of family life to be more adversely affected in Chichester than in Salisbury during the two years follow up. At two years the difference was significant for two of the items: families in Chichester were left with more financial problems and the effect on the mental health of family members was also greater (P < 0.01). The impaired mental health of family members in the community service is an observation of considerable importance, and inevitably obliges us to consider whether the cost of keeping certain patients at home will be more mental illness in the community. The effect on children was very likely underestimated as we relied on the parents' description of them; but during the two years only 2% in each district were referred to a child guidance clinic and 9% in each developed clearly neurotic symptoms; 8% of the school children in Chichester and 3% in Salisbury had had time away from school; and 33% in Chichester and 23% in Salisbury had become disturbed (backward at school, unduly naughty etc.), due, the family said, to the patient's illness. While it appears that a high proportion of children may be affected by mental illness in their parents, there is little evidence from these data that the service which admits more patients to hospital is more successful in protecting children [8].

Our first conclusion was that 'community care' as practised in Chichester left the families with more problems than did the more conservative hospital-based policy. What was this increased social cost due to, and to what extent is it preventable? Further analyses gave some indications.

3. Changes in family burden during two years

Table 7.1 showed that when first referred, the problems incurred by families in the two areas did not differ. But a comparison with their situations *one month later* showed that contact with either of the services had had an immediate effect in relieving family burden (see table 7.3). At this time both services were equally effective in relieving burden when it was *severe*, but not when it was less marked, because more families in Salisbury who had been rated as having *some* burden were relieved. This advantage to Salisbury families was a trend consistently maintained in all social and clinical groups.

After two years, the community service in spite of admitting fewer patients, again equalled the hospital-based one in the relief it gave to severely burdened families but not in the relief to those in which the burden was less marked (rated 'some'). We therefore modified our first conclusion: although the hospital service was more successful than the community one in helping moderately burdened families, the severely burdened were equally relieved in both services.

We have already shown that the problems of a family with a mentally ill member depend on his symptoms, his age and so on, but they will also depend on whether the patient gets admitted, and whether the family receives the social support needed to cope with them. So next we looked at the relation of these factors to relief of family burden.

Although the elderly had caused most problems, the families of a psycho-geriatric patient were equally relieved in both services (see table 7.6), but the families of young patients were relieved more in Salisbury. Our statement that families in the community service had more problems therefore needs qualifying further—the extra relief given to families in the hospital-based service was confined not just to the moderately burdened households, but also to those with patients under 65. Conversely the failure to relieve families of their problems in the community was limited to those with younger patients and then was largely independent of their diagnosis.

TABLE 7.6 **Percentage of families relieved of burden after two years**

	Chichester %	Salisbury %
Patients aged:		
*15–64 years	55	82
65+ years	74	80

* $P < 0.01$.

But symptoms that the family found most worrying (see table 7.5) are more important to consider than diagnosis. When the families who were still troubled by problems of the patients' behaviour were compared in Chichester and Salisbury after two years, we found that those contending with the more socially disturbing symptoms such as dangerous or suicidal behaviour were equally relieved in both, but families of patients with less socially conspicuous behaviour were relieved significantly more in Salisbury. Once more it is only when the effect on the family is obvious and manifest that the community service rises to the occasion.

Relief of burden and admission to hospital
Although the patients referred were well matched clinically and socially, significantly more were admitted *at some time during the two years* in Salisbury (59%) than in Chichester (38%). Conse-

quently many patients in Chichester remained at home who would have been admitted in Salisbury. To what extent were those patients responsible for the extra burden on families in Chichester?

When the burden ratings in the two services were compared at the two-years follow-up, the patients who had never been admitted had *not* inflicted more hardship in the community than in the hospital-based service. On the other hand those patients who had been admitted at some time during the two years were causing significantly more burden to their families in the community service; moreover, only 59% of the families of *admitted* patients were relieved of burden, whereas in the hospital service 87% were. But families of patients *treated at home* were relieved to a similar extent in both services. Failure to admit therefore is not the factor which accounts for the greater impairment found in Chichester households; on the contrary it was the patients who had been admitted at some time who were responsible.

When this latter group were examined, those who were the source of their families' troubles were the young, mostly neurotic, depressed and hypochondriacal patients, whose effects on their families had not been conspicuous or severe but unequivocal nevertheless. (The families of admissions who were elderly or who had been a severe burden were equally relieved in both services.)

Burden and social work
The likely reason for this somewhat paradoxical finding is that more social support was given to patients and their families in Salisbury. This explanation not only imposes some order on a number of other findings, but also draws attention to what the success or failure of a community service must depend on—close co-operation between the psychiatric and the social and welfare services.

Our records show that the patients in Chichester and Salisbury received comparable psychiatric treatment, but when the amount of social help given to them and their families were compared, much more was done in Salisbury.

In the Chichester service the psychiatrist visited the patient's home and he assessed their circumstances and needs without the expert help of a psychiatric social worker. The psychiatrist apparently recognized the more obviously burdened families and the more conspicuous problems the patient imposed; and dealt with them. But the more covert difficulties and needs of families were missed, and therefore often neglected. In Salisbury, by contrast, although the service was hospital-based, there was a better staffed social work department which assigned a case worker to each new patient, and then maintained active contact with both the patient and his family. Consequently more social work of every kind was given.

This difference between the services in the amount of social case work and practical help provided can be clearly seen when the estimates of needs that the research social workers made at their first visit and the work that was in fact done during the two years are compared in Chichester and in Salisbury (see table 7.7); nearly six times as many families were helped in Salisbury.

TABLE 7.7 **Social work done in the two services**

Type of Work	%Patients Chichester (186)	65 years Salisbury (105)	%Patients Chichester (85)	65+ years Salisbury (34)
Social assessment made	8	38	5	21
Support, advice or case-work given	5	36	7	26
Help with employment problems	6	17	0	3
Rehabilitation arranged	1	15	0	0
Help with housing or money problems	9	15	6	12
Help with children or domestic problems	2	7	1	0
Institutional placement	2	1	12	6

The categories of patients that did as well in the community as in the control service were the elderly and the severely disturbed; it was only these groups who were given social and welfare help on a scale comparable to that in Salisbury. Similarly, it was the severely burdened families in Chichester who were given most clinical support and they obtained the same degree of relief as the severely burdened in Salisbury. The patients and their families who fared worse were those whose burden was rated as moderate. Their needs were neither identified nor met, whereas their counterparts in Salisbury were routinely seen by the social worker in collaboration with the psychiatrist. Thus, the young neurotics and character disorders, who were admitted in Chichester at some time during the two years and then discharged to the out-patient clinic or day-hospital, were not followed up at home nor were the problems inflicted on their families systematically examined.

Outcome in the community service, whether in terms of social cost to the patient, such as amount of time spent in full-time work (many more remained unemployed in Chichester), or in terms of social cost to the family was worse than in Salisbury in those categories of patients and households that received least help.

Discussion and Conclusions

In order to evaluate the effects of treating patients in the community, all referrals to a service whose policy was to treat patients at home as far as possible were compared with those to a more conservative hospital-centred one. And the burden on the families of a cohort of patients, who were followed up for two years, was assessed. The patients' studies therefore covered the whole range of psychiatric referrals from severe psychotics to those seen for an opinion and not diagnosed as ill. Nevertheless, the social cost to their families was found to be high in both services, and one that had been borne for more than two years in over half. Even after two years of being in contact with the services 20% of the families were still burdened.

The social cost of psychiatric care was higher in the community than in the hospital-based service. This was principally due to the greater burden caused by a group of patients who are not usually retained in hospital even in a service that preferentially admits. The strain on their families was not being recognized because it was not prominent. So our findings emphasize the importance of supplementing the clinical care of a patient treated outside hospital with a systematic appraisal of the demands being made on the family and then providing them with adequate social support. Without efficiently organized collaboration between the psychiatric and welfare services both the patient and those in the community closest to him are likely to entail costs—financial, social and emotional. Thus the observation that the effects on the mental health of family members were worse in the community than in the comparison service must sound a note of caution.

Nevertheless, since the biggest demand is beds for geriatric patients, and since they presented the most severe problems to their families, the success of the community service in reducing this demand without increasing family burden is noteworthy, and suggests that our findings cannot be interpreted as a condemnation of community care policy. The Chichester service was able to match the Salisbury one when clinical care was backed by social case work and family needs were met. Similarly, the tendency to give preferential admission to patients in Chichester whose families' burdens and social problems were marked also indicates that by careful assessment it is possible in a community service to select the most suitable of a number of alternative types of care; and determine which one brings most advantage to both the patient and his family. By the same token, better opportunities for discharge can obviate the chronic impairment which is associated with a prolonged period in the mental hospital.

There are other findings on the credit side. Firstly, that the kind of disposal given in the community service was more in keeping with the families' wishes than that given in the hospital-centred one. And our agreed impression was that many families prefer to care for their sick patients at home even though it entails hardships. Secondly, that the general practitioners favoured the extramural policy even though the cost in their time and extra work was significantly greater [9].

Finally, in other respects the community service had beneficial effects and was more efficient in that it met needs more effectively: extending services in this way increased the referral rates of patients, especially the elderly, those with serious disorders, the socially disadvantaged, and those groups known to be most at risk for suicide; people were also seen earlier on in their illness. This indicates the very considerable preventive potential that community psychiatric services have in reducing the harmful effects and cost in human suffering of mental illness.

References

1. Kreitman, N., Sainsbury, P., Morrissey, J., Towers, J. and Scrivener, J., *Journal of Mental Science*, *107*, 887–908, 1961

2. Tizard, J. and Grad, J. C., 'The Mentally Handicapped and their Families', *Maudsley Monograph*, No. 7, London, 1961

3. May, P. R. A., *Treatment of Schizophrenia*, New York, 1968

4. Walk, D., *British Journal of Psychiatry*, *113*, 1381–92, 1967

5. Barraclough, B., *Social Science and Medicine*, *6*, 661–71, 1972

6. Grad, J. C. and Sainsbury, P., *Milbank Memorial Fund Quarterly*, *44*, part 2, 231–77, 1966

7. Grad, J. C. and Sainsbury, P., *Lancet*, *i*, 544–47, 1963

8. Grad, J. C. and Sainsbury, P., *British Journal of Psychiatry*, *114*, 265–78, 1968

9. Sainsbury, P. and Grad de Alarcon, J., *Journal of Geriatric Psychiatry*, *4*, 23–41, 1970

8 Impairment and Disability: Their Measurement, Prevalence and Psychological Cost[1]

J. GARRAD

DEFINITIONS OF IMPAIRMENT AND DISABILITY

'When *I* use a word,' Humpty Dumpty said, 'it means just what I chose it to mean—neither more nor less'.

'The question is,' said Alice, 'whether you *can* make words mean different things'.

'The question is,' said Humpty Dumpty, 'which is to be master—that's all'.

It is unlikely that either Alice or Humpty Dumpty engaged in studies of impairment and disability but I suggest that Humpty Dumpty's precision in the use of words would make him the better research worker in this field which is fraught with terminological difficulties.

My medical colleague, Dr A. E. Bennett, and I conducted a series of studies in relation to our interest in the provision of health and social services. Our first task was to define our terms [9].

The popular concept of a disabled person is of someone who has lost a limb or who is physically deformed in some obvious

---

1 The studies discussed here were undertaken when I was Lecturer in the Department of Clinical Epidemiology and Social Medicine at St. Thomas's Hospital Medical School, London, and I should like to acknowledge my indebtedness to Professor W. W. Holland. Many members of the Department made valued contributions to these studies which were supported by the Endowment Funds of St. Thomas's Hospital, The Department of Health and Social Security, the South West Metropolitan Regional Hospital Board and the City Parochial Charities.

way. This concept is largely based on the appreciation of structural damage; severity is considered to be dependent on the extent of the damage and criteria based on this approach govern the assessment and award of the disability pensions at present available. However, disability may be thought of in terms of behaviour and performance and may be considered as limitation of the performance of an individual when compared with a 'fit' person. This concept considers disability as a disorder of function rather than a structural abnormality or loss. In America, reports of the Committee on the Medical Rating of Physical Impairment [5] distinguish between these two approaches. The concept of the total functional loss is considered to be disability whereas the anatomical or structural abnormality is described as impairment.

We adopted this distinction but defined these two terms more strictly. We defined *impairment* as an anatomical, pathological or psychological disorder which may be described in diagnostic or symptomatic terms. It may cause or be associated with disability so that while every disabled person has an impairment, not all people with impairments are necessarily disabled. Impairments may be classified into four categories: those affecting locomotion or any motor activity; those of sensory origin; those referable to internal medicine, e.g. cardiac and respiratory disorders; and those of primarily psychological origin together with unclassifiable organic disorder. We defined *disability* as limitation of performance in one or more activities which are generally accepted as essential basic components of daily living, such that inability to perform them necessitates dependence on another person. The severity of disability is thus proportional to the degree of dependence. The areas of essential activity are (1) mobility: walking, negotiating stairs, transfer in and out of bed or chair, and travel; (2) self-care: feeding, dressing and toilet care; (3) domestic duties: shopping, preparation and cooking of food, household cleaning, and washing of clothes; and/or (4) occupation: the ability to hold unmodified employment in open industry consistent with the individual's age, sex and skill.

We emphasize the dynamic nature of this conceptual model of disability. An infant born 'fit' and continuing to survive will progress to become impaired and subsequently disabled. The usual sequence of events is for the period of 'fitness' to end in middle age or later with the manifestation of one or more of the chronic degenerative diseases, most commonly of locomotor or internal origin. As the disease progresses the individual loses his independence of living and thereafter becomes increasingly disabled. However, for each individual the time periods of the different stages will vary. Following the onset of diseases such as rheumatoid arthritis or multiple sclerosis, the period of disability may extend to many years, whereas after a severe stroke or the onset of some malignant condition the period may be short. An infant born with a congenital abnormality is impaired and possibly disabled throughout life. A child involved in an accident may lose a limb and be impaired for life but may only become disabled when the effects of ageing supervene. Death is an event which at some point intervenes to prevent further progression. Acute illness with cure or recovery from a chronic condition both show how the model need not be considered unremittingly progressive, even in the short term.

The critical point in the progression is when independence of living is lost and disability ensues. Obviously this is not as sharp a point of demarcation in all cases as would be desired for the purposes of measurement. If acute illness is excluded by setting a minimum time qualification such as three months, factors causing oscillation at this point are changes in severity of the disease or changes in the psychological state of the patient. If these are liable to fluctuate then the individual's ability to perform tasks unaided may vary. Thus an individual's classification may change as his performance changes, from, say, minimally disabled to impaired only or vice versa; or from one level of severity of disability to another.

However, in the same way as fluctuation or remission in the severity of a disease process allows independence to be regained, so may treatment restore the necessary function. The objectives of surgical procedures or use of gadgets are all similar in attempting to restore and maintain the ability of the individual to function independently, or to function to the best of limited abilities.

MEASUREMENT OF DISABILITY

There are three main methods by which disability defined in functional terms can be identified and measured. The first of these is by clinical assessment of the individual's performance. Un-

I.D.H.—6*

fortunately, however, it has been shown that observers of different professional disciplines use different criteria for assessing performance [17]. Moreover, perception of change in an individual's performance is related to the observer's role in the treatment and assessment situation [27]. If an attempt is made to overcome these difficulties by forming a team of several clinical disciplines to make the assessment, unanimity is unlikely. The options then are either to accept democratically the majority opinion, to 'weight' the opinions of the various observers or to accept that the leader of the team has the prerogative to resolve any difference [17]. These difficulties are more easily resolved in the clinical situation, and the method presents considerable organizational problems for large-scale surveys.

The second principal method involves the use of standard tests of performance by the individual conducted by an observer trained in the administration of the test. Examples are the Maryland Disability Index, also known as the Barthel Index [30], and the Index of A.D.L. [16]. In these scales, a number of activities are defined which an individual must be able to complete unaided in order to live an independent life. The individual's performance is observed and his level of independence in each activity is rated according to carefully defined criteria. In a variation of this method, the individual is tested for his ability to make the basic movements needed to perform these activities rather than his ability to perform the activities [15].

However, with any tests of performance the problem of the effect of interaction between the individual, the observer, and the test situation is important [29; 23; 26; 4]. Kelman and Willner [17] obtained three different scores when patients resident in a nursing home were rated under three different sets of conditions: in non-test, day-to-day conditions in the nursing home rated by staff familiar to them; in a test situation in their nursing home rated by staff familiar to them; and in a test situation outside their nursing home rated by unknown staff. In general, the test situation outside the nursing home with unfamiliar observers produced the lowest ratings. However, some patients appeared to be so stimulated by the novelty of the strange situation as to perform better: this phenomenon was also reported by Muller [22].

Closely associated with the variation in performance due to rapport between individual and observer and the effect of the test situation is the factor of the individual's self-concept. Litman

[*19*] has shown that patients' progress in rehabilitation is largely dependent on their self-concept. If they consider themselves to be capable of playing a definite, although altered, role in society, they respond better to treatment than if they consider themselves as disabled and limited people. It is arguable that a person's performance in a test situation would be affected in a similar way. Another component of the individual's motivation which may affect performance is the secondary gain which he thinks may result from performing well or badly.

The third method by which disability defined in functional terms may be measured is by questioning the individual as to his current level of daily performance. Communication difficulties and confusional states may render this method impossible or unreliable. For this reason Sett [*25*], in his questionnaire, included a section to assess communication and mental state which is administered first and, if necessary, the remainder of the questionnaire is then administered to a relative or member of the nursing staff. When the respondent answers for himself, problems of self-concept and secondary gain are also relevant in this method.

DEVELOPMENT OF SURVEY TECHNIQUES

We designed and tested a structured interview schedule. Section I of the interview schedule identifies and assesses the severity of disability and Section II classifies the impairment and identifies the principal diagnostic group. The validity and reliability of these sections were finally determined by comparison with clinical records and repeated use after intervals of up to one year.

Section I: Assessment of disability

Criteria to identify disability in each essential activity of daily living and the different levels of severity were at first arbitrarily set from clinical experience. The questionnaire was tested on a wide range of inpatients and outpatients for meaningfulness, intelligibility, and acceptability. It was repeatedly modified and retested until satisfactory wording and grading were obtained (see Figs. 8.1 and 8.2).

Criteria for disability are: walking less than $\frac{1}{4}$ mile unaccompanied; walking up or down less than nine stairs unaccompanied;

FIGURE 8.1

SECTION I

MOBILITY

Walking Do you walk outdoors in the street (with crutch or stick if used)?

If 'Yes': one mile or more	[ ]	If 'No':		and:	
¼ mile	[ ]	Between rooms	[*]	Unaccompanied	[ ]
100 yds.	[*]	Within room	[*]	Accompanied	[*]
10 yds.	[*]	Unable to walk	[*]	Acc.+support	[*]

Stairs Do you walk up stairs? | Do you walk down stairs?

To 1st floor or above	[ ]			From 1 floor to another	[ ]		
5–8 steps or stairs	[*]	Unacc.	[ ]	5–8 steps or stairs	[*]	Unacc.	[ ]
2–4 steps or stairs	[*]	Acc.	[*]	2–4 steps or stairs	[*]	Acc.	[*]
1 step	[*]	Acc. & Supp.	[*]	1 step	[*]	Acc. & Supp.	[*]
mount stairs other than by walking	[*]	No need to mount stairs	[ ]	goes down stairs other than by walking	[*]	No need to descend stairs	[ ]
unable to mount stairs	[*]			unable to descend stairs	[*]		

Transfer

	Yes	No		Yes	No
Do you need help to get into bed?	[*]	[ ]	Do you need help to sit down in a chair?	[*]	[ ]
Do you need help to get out of bed?	[*]	[ ]	Do you need help to stand up from a chair?	[*]	[ ]
Bedfast	[*]		Not applicable	[ ]	

Travel

Do you drive yourself in a car? | Do you travel by bus or train?

		If 'Yes':		If 'No':	
Normal (unadapt.)	[ ]	Whenever necessary	[ ]	Unable to use bus and train	[*]
Adapted	[ ]	Only out of rush hour	[*]	Unable to use bus, train and car	[*]
Invacar	[*]	and:			
Self-propelled vehicle (outdoors)	[*]	Unaccompanied	[ ]	Does not travel by choice	[ ]
Does not drive	[ ]	Accompanied	[*]	Uses private transport by choice	[ ]

FIGURE 8.2

SELF CARE

Are you able to feed yourself:	Are you able to dress yourself completely:	Are you able to undress yourself completely:	Are you able to use the lavatory:	Are you able to wash yourself:
Without any help ☐	Without any help ☐	Without any help ☐	Without any help ☐	Without any help ☐
With specially prepared food or containers ✶	With help with fastenings ✶	With help with fastenings ✶	Receptacles without assistance ✶	With assistance for shaving, combing hair, etc. ✶
With assistance ✶	With help other than fastenings ✶	With help other than fastenings ✶	Lavatory with assistance ✶	With help for bodily washing ✶
Not at all, must be fed ✶	Does not dress ✶	Not applicable ✶	Receptacles with assistance ✶	Not at all ✶

DOMESTIC DUTIES Do you do your own:

	all	part	none	preference	unable
Shopping	☐	☐	☐	☐	✶
Cooking	☐	☐	☐	☐	✶
Cleaning	☐	☐	☐	☐	✶
Clothes washing	☐	☐	☐	☐	✶
Men with no household duties	☐				

OCCUPATION Do you have a paid job at present?

If 'Yes':	and:	If 'No':

Full time ☐

Part-time ☐

Normal working ☐

Modified working ✶

Sheltered employment ✶

Males 65 Females 60 and over
- Age retired ☐
- Prem. retired ✶
- Non-employed ☐

Males 64 Female 59 and under
- Unemployed ☐
- Unfit ✶
- Non-employed ☐

✶ Cross in any box marked with an asterisk indicates presence of disability.

needing help to get in or out of bed or chair; using an invacar or self-propelled vehicle outdoors; inability to travel by public transport unaccompanied whenever necessary; needing special facilities for feeding; needing assistance with personal washing; inability to perform all the defined domestic duties; inability to undertake unmodified employment if of working age, or having retired prematurely on medical grounds if currently over retirement age. Initially, if an individual met any one of these criteria he or she was classified as disabled. However, it became apparent that all the same criteria could not meaningfully be applied to people aged 65 or over, especially in the area of travel and domestic duties. Therefore, for this age group only, these criteria were modified to accept a lower level of performance as adequate and not indicative of disability. For the majority of men over 65 occupation does not demand the ability to travel on public transport unaccompanied at any time, so this criterion, applicable to the younger age groups, was relaxed. For women over 65 domestic duties become more onerous and many women are not able to maintain their levels of activity. Since there is in the performance of domestic duties a large qualitative component, the criteria for those over 65 were relaxed so that accomplishment of only part of the household duties did not imply disability as it did in the younger age groups.

Many rating scales present a score calculated as an algebraic sum of the component scores and this presents problems as it masks different levels of performance, resulting in loss of information. Ekwall [6] reviews several methods of assessing disability in which 'socio-medical' and 'psycho-social' factors are considered to be relevant variables. A particular value of his paper lies in a description of the method whereby a large amount of data is quantified and summarized without such loss. We adopted a similar method of scoring to quantify the level of performance in each essential activity of daily living and designed a method of coding the information for data processing. Each individual is described by four scores, one for each area of essential activity, and these scores may be presented as a profile.

Section II: Identification of impairment

A locomotor impairment was identified by four questions enquiring for permanent paralysis or weakness of specified parts of the body—by pain and by limitation of movement in specified joints. The interviewer noted tremor of hands and/or speech interference and recorded any comments volunteered by the respondent. A sensory impairment was identified by questions devised to assess loss of hearing, defective vision, loss of tactile sense or appreciation of temperature and disturbance of balance. The subsection for internal impairments consisted partly of the questionnaire on respiratory symptoms [20] and part of the questionnaire for the diagnosis of ischaemic heart pain [24] with additional questions designed to identify conditions such as diabetes.

POPULATION SURVEYS

Method

In 1966 and 1967 we undertook a two-stage epidemiological survey [2]. Initially a private census of a 20% random sample of dwellings in the six northern wards of Lambeth was taken and each enumerated person born before 1 January 1951—that is, aged $15\frac{1}{2}$ and over—was asked to complete a short self-administered questionnaire.[1] This contained 15 questions, of which 10 related to disability and impairment; each required a 'yes' or 'no' answer. Four questions asked whether the respondent could perform four essential activities of daily living without help, and a fifth whether there were limitation in *any* daily activities. Five questions inquired for selected physical impairments which might seriously affect locomotor activity and be associated with disability. The remaining five questions concerned personal and occupational data.

For the second stage an age-sex stratified sample of males and females aged 35–74 was drawn from those identified as disabled and impaired or impaired only. This gave a study population of 260 males and 311 females, and they were matched for age and sex with non-disabled non-impaired controls giving a total sample of 1,142.

Each respondent was visited at home and the validated inter-

---

[1] The basic idea underlying the Lambeth studies is described in [12].

view schedule was administered. Data was obtained on 1,026 respondents. Seventeen interviewers took part, each having received training for some three weeks before starting field-work. Each completed interview schedule was reviewed by one of us on the day after the interview and checked for completeness and internal consistency. At regular intervals completed interview schedules were reviewed with the interviewers and their performance checked.

Prevalence of disability

We found a prevalence of disability of 7.2% for males and 9.7% for females, increasing from under 5% for those aged 35–44 to over 20% for those of 65–74 (see table 8.1).

TABLE 8.1   **Final estimates of percentages of disabled males and females living in Lambeth**

Study	Sex	Age in Years				All Ages
		35–44	*45–54*	*55–64*	*65–74*	
Final Estimate	Males	0·6[1]	4·0	11·4	20·4	7·2
% Disabled	Females	4·1[1]	7·1	11·1	20·8	9·7

[1] Difference between sexes statistically significant $P < 0.05$.

The female excess was contributed by the younger age groups and largely reflected limited ability to perform domestic duties. These activities are not relevant for most men and so were not included in the assessment of their disability in most cases. Males may be more fortunate in being able to undertake physically less demanding activities in full-time open employment.

Associated impairments

The estimated percentages of disabled people according to the category of the primary impairment associated with their disability are given in Table 8.2:

TABLE 8.2 **Estimated percentages of primary impairment categories associated with disability in males and females aged 35–74 years**

Sex		Impairment Category				All Categories
		Locomotor	Sensory	Internal	Other	
Males	%	2·5	0·1	3·5	1·1	7·2
Females	%	5·1	0·6	2·8	1·2	9·7

The major diagnostic groups within the locomotor and internal impairment categories are given in Table 8.3:

TABLE 8.3 **Estimated percentages of primary diagnoses associated with disability in males and females aged 35–74 years**

Sex	Locomotor Impairment		Internal Impairment	
	Cerebro-vascular Disease	Arthritic Disease	Respiratory Disease	Cardio-vascular Disease
Males	0·6	0·8	2·3	0·8
Females	0·4	1·7	1·1	0·9

For females there is an excess of locomotor impairments, particularly arthritic disease. For both sexes cerebrovascular disease with paralysis is the next major contributor of locomotor impairment, and the remainder of the category is composed of other nervous diseases, such as multiple sclerosis and epilepsy, and various disorders of bones and joints, such as amputation and congenital malformation. Sensory impairments, which form the smallest category, are almost all due to blindness or defective vision: internal impairments are mainly due to respiratory and cardiovascular disease. The fourth category of other impairments contains predominantly psychological disorder. Chronic respiratory disease, principally bronchitis, is the single most important diagnostic group associated with disability when males and females are considered together.

Discussion

We show that 7.2% of males and 9.7% of females aged 35–74 living in the community are disabled according to our definition. It is difficult to compare our estimates with other data for there are so few and definitions differ. Our data, however, are in close agreement with the findings of the Danish study [3] which identified 6.5% of persons aged 15–61 as 'physically handicapped'. Jeffreys et al. [15] found that 3.4% of the population aged 16 and over 'could be described as motor impaired' and as many as 6% may have some level of such impairment. In America a survey of chronic illness found that 2.7% of the population of all ages suffered from chronic conditions which limited mobility [28]. We describe 2.5% of men and 5.1% of women aged 35–74 as being disabled with an associated locomotor impairment. Harris [11] published the results of a national survey in Great Britain. Inconsistencies in the use of terminology make her data difficult to interpret but she quotes 6.7% of men and 8.8% of women aged 16 and over as having some 'impairment'. Although superficially similar to ours, these rates apply to a different age group and more detailed comparisons suggest that different populations have been identified [1]. Harris (op. cit.) does not include those people with psychological impairment or with mixed physical and psychological impairment; but she has a higher proportion of respondents with locomotor impairment—perhaps due to a bias in sampling introduced by the wording of the screening questionnaire.

Our data describing the categories of the impairments and the diagnostic groups of the impairments among the disabled population are, we believe, unique as they were obtained by use of a validated schedule. They can therefore be assessed only in the light of other knowledge. Internal impairments, almost entirely due to respiratory and cardiovascular disease, are more prevalent in males than in females. By contrast locomotor impairments are more prevalent in females, and both these differences are in the direction expected from a knowledge of the prevalence of the individual conditions. Respiratory disease is the diagnostic group making the largest contribution to disability in males and females together, and again this finding would seem in accord with disease prevalence and the natural history of the pathological process. The estimates of disability associated with sensory impairment are in broad agreement with the numbers of blind and partially sighted persons on the register of the then Welfare Department of the Lambeth Borough Council, which also shows a similar excess of females.

We have been careful in describing the impairment as being associated with disability. In most cases there is little doubt that this is a direct causal association and the functional loss is the result of anatomical or pathological change. In some cases, however, the disability may result from unidentified psychological illness and be mistakenly ascribed to organic disease present at the same time. For these reasons we hesitate to describe a simple cause-and-effect relationship for all cases.

PSYCHOLOGICAL STUDIES

Following these studies I undertook a further series of studies in 1968 and 1969 when I made more detailed psychological investigations on subsamples of the 1967 population [8]. I obtained data using Fould's Personal Disturbance Scale [7], Goldberg's General Health Questionnaire [10] and sections of the Minnesota Multiphasic Personality Inventory [21]. The data show that there is a gradient in the prevalence of psychological disturbance as identified by these validated psychometric scales, being highest among disabled respondents, lower among those who have an impairment but are not disabled and lowest among those who do not have an impairment. The difference in prevalence of psychological disturbance between the disabled group and the impaired but not disabled group is highly significant statistically when the data are standardized for age and sex. The question arises whether the onset of psychological disturbance follows the development of disability (and may perhaps be a consequence of it) or whether the presence of psychological disturbance in individuals suffering an impairment leads to the development of disability, perhaps by reducing motivation to perform independently. When the data are analysed by the method described by Ibrahim et al. [13; 14] the findings suggest that the psychological disturbance follows the onset of disability. From these studies therefore, I conclude that in psychological terms the disabled group and the impaired only group are two populations showing different psychological characteristics.

When I was practising as a medical social worker in the clinical situation I became interested in the effect that chronic illness or disability exerted on the individual's relationships with the spouse and other family members. So in these psychological studies, I included a pilot study to identify the areas requiring further investigation. Among other findings, this showed that the wives of disabled men aged 45–64 have a higher prevalence of psychological disturbance than the wives of a control group of men suffering the same range of impairments but who were not disabled. I take this as further evidence of psychological differences between disabled and impaired-only populations.

Conclusions

The two concepts of disability and impairment are of practical value as they can be defined and therefore attempts can be made to measure them. In the first stage of these studies 1,621 men and women out of the total population of 13,903 reported one or more of the specified impairments. Of the 1,621 impaired individuals only 582 (35.9%) reported disability. The fact that 64.1% of the impaired group was not disabled underlines the distinction drawn in the definitions.

Not only is the separation of the two concepts of practical value, but it reveals the existence of two populations with different psychological characteristics. If the prevalence of psychological disturbance is a measure of psychological cost, then the psychological cost of disability is significantly higher than the cost of impairment. Furthermore, a follow-up study in 1970, showed that over a two-year period the standardized death rate for those people identified as disabled in the 1967 survey was increased 5-fold over that of the whole population of the same geographical area, revealing an additional cost in terms of reduced life expectancy.

Finally, these studies enable the identification of at-risk groups: people suffering an impairment are at risk of becoming disabled: people who are disabled by physical impairments are at risk of developing psychological disturbance. The identification of at-risk groups enables planning for the provision of appropriate preventive medical and para-medical services. While these would constitute a new item of cost, effective services would reduce subsequent financial, social and psychological costs.

References

1. Bennett, A. E., 'Disability: The Problem in the Community', *Proceedings of the Royal Society of Medicine*, *65*, 202, 1972

2. Bennett, A. E., Garrad, J. and Halil, T., 'Chronic disease and disability in the community: a prevalence study, *British Medical Journal*, *3*, 762, 1970

3. Bonnevie, P., *Ugeskrift for Laeger*, *128*, 1199, 1966

4. Cole, S. L. and Griffith, G. C., 'Assay of antianginal agents—the rapport period', *Journal of the American Medical Association*, *168*, 275, 1958

5. Committee on the Medical Rating of Physical Impairment, 'A guide to the evaluation of permanent impairment of the extremities and back', *Journal of the American Medical Association*, *166*, 15 February 1958

6. Ekwall, B., 'Method for evaluating indications for rehabilitation in chronic hemiplegia', *Acta Medica Scandinavica*, Suppl. 450, 1966

7. Foulds, G. A., *Personality and Personal Illness*, London, Tavistock Publications, 1965

8. Garrad, J., In preparation

9. Garrad, J. and Bennett, A. E. 'A validated interview schedule for use in population surveys of chronic disease and disability', *British Journal of Preventive and Social Medicine*, *25*, No. 2, 97, 1971

10. Goldberg, D. P. and Blackwell, B., 'Psychiatric illness in general practice. A detailed study using a new method of case identification', *British Medical Journal*, *1*, 439, 1970

11. Harris, A. I., *Handicapped and Impaired in Great Britain*, Part 1, London, HMSO, 1971

12. Holland, W. W. and Waller, J., 'Population studies in the Borough of Lambeth', *Community Medicine*, *126*, No. 11 (pp. 153–56)

13. Ibrahim, M. A., Jenkins, C. D., Cassel, J. C., McDonough, J. R. and Harnes, C. G., 'Personality traits and coronary heart disease. Utilization of a cross-sectional study design to test whether a selected psychological profile precedes or follows manifest coronary heart disease', *Journal of Chronic Diseases*, *19*, 255, 1966

14. Ibrahim, M. A., Sackett, D. L., Kantor S. and Winkelstein, W., 'Psychological patterns and coronary heart disease: an appraisal of the determination of etiology by means of a stochastic process', *Journal of Chronic Diseases*, *20*, 931, 1968

15. Jefferys, M., Millard, J. B., Hyman, M. and Warren, M. S., 'A set of tests for measuring motor impairment in prevalence studies', *Journal of Chronic Diseases*, 22, 303, 1969

16. Katz, S., Ford, A. B., Moskowitz, R. W., Jackson, B. A. and Jaffe, M. W., 'Studies of illness in the aged', *Journal of the American Medical Association*, 185, 914, 1963

17. Kelman, H. R. and Willner, A., 'Problems in measurement and evaluation of rehabilitation', *Archives of Physical Medicine*, 43, 172, 1962

18. Litman, T. J., 'The influence of self conception and life orientation factors in the rehabilitation of the orthopedically disabled', *Journal of Health and Human Behaviour*, 3, 249, 1962

19. Litman, T. J., 'An analysis of the sociologic factors affecting the rehabilitation of physically handicapped patients', *Archives of Physical Medicine*, 45, 9, 1964

20. Medical Research Council, 'A questionnaire on respiratory symptoms approved by the MRC Committee on Research into Chronic Bronchitis', 1966

21. Minnesota Multiphasic Personality Inventory, *Basic readings on the MMPI in Psychology and Medicine*, University of Minnesota Press, Minneapolis, 1960

22. Muller, J. N., 'Rehabilitation evaluation—some social and clinical problems', *American Journal of Public Health*, 51, 403, 1961

23. Osgood, C. E. and Suci, G. J., 'A measure of relation determined by both mean difference and profile information', *Psychological Bulletin*, 49, 251, 1952

24. Rose, G. A., 'The diagnosis of ischaemic heart pain and intermittent claudication in field surveys', *Bulletin of World Health Organization*, 27, 645, 1962

25. Sett, R. F., 'Simplified tests for evaluation of patients with chronic illness (cerebro-vascular accidents)', *Journal of American Geriatric Society*, 11, 1095, 1963

26. Shontz, F. C. and Fink, S. L., 'The significance of patient-staff rapport in the rehabilitation of individuals with chronic physical illness', *Journal of Consultant Psychology*, 21, 327, 1957

27. Tamerin, J. S., 'The perception of progress in rehabilitation', *Archives of Physical Medicine*, 45, 17, 1964

28. US National Center for Health Statistics, *Vital and Health Statistics*, Series 10, No. 9, 1964

29. Wolf, S., 'Effects of suggestion and conditioning on the action of chemical agents in human subjects: the pharmacology of placebos', *Journal of Clinical Investigation*, 29, 100, 1950

30. Wylie, C. M. and White, B. K., 'A measure of disability', *Archives of Environmental Health*, 8, 834, 1964

9 The Development of a Classification of the Symptoms of Sickness and its use to Measure the Output of a Hospital

R. M. ROSSER and V. C. WATTS

Introduction

One of the principal objectives of health services is to alter the natural progress of change in symptoms. The assessment of the extent to which this objective is achieved with individual patients is intrinsic to clinical method. These assessments are detailed and cannot be readily aggregated to provide summary statements about the achievements of a health service. Summary statements providing information on the extent to which health service achieves 'health end results' would permit comparisons of the improvements in health across disease classes and across specialties and would consequently be of use for evaluation [*1; 2; 5*]. The development of general measures of health and results has been reviewed by Fanshel and Bush [*3*].

The measures described here have been developed from the viewpoint of the patient. Therefore, the effect of symptoms on the patient's functional and emotional state is emphasized and their aetiology, which is primarily of interest to the clinician, is ignored. The context of the study was a District General Hospital.

When a patient seeks treatment, it is assumed that he wants an improvement in his present and future functional and emotional state. The success of his treatment is related to the difference between his state of disability and distress at the commencement and at the end of treatment. Continuing descriptions of the patient's disability and distress at intervals after the end of the episode of treatment could be used to measure the change in his longer term state of health.

If the state of disability and distress of all patients treated by a health service are classified on a common basis, it becomes possible to add up the individual changes, and thus to make quantitative statements about the achievements of this particular service. In the study described in the next section a classification of disability and distress was developed and used to measure the changes which occurred in the symptoms of patients treated in a general hospital.

The classification described has eight states of disability and four states of distress. Consequently the summary statements which quantify the changes occurring in the states of the patients involve many numbers. It would be convenient to summarize these changes in a few numbers and this could be done if a scale were to be developed to weight the relative importance of these various changes in disability and distress. The methods by which such a scale might be developed and the results of using one of these methods, are discussed in Section 3 (page 166 *seq.*).

The elements of changes in present and future states of sickness and the transformations required for their scaling have been analysed mathematically elsewhere [7].

The classification of functional and emotional state and its use in a general hospital

The study was done at St. Olave's Hospital (297 beds), a general hospital which became part of the Guy's Hospital Group in 1967. During the latter part of 1971, progressive patient care was introduced into the hospital. The purpose of this change was to improve the quality of in-patient care and several studies have been designed to help in quantifying the change and the costs associated with this. In particular, the studies concerned with end results involved the following:

1. Sanative Output—the effect of the hospital on the immediate health of its patients.
2. Long Term Output—the effect of the hospital on the long term health of its patients.
3. Mortality.
4. Patient satisfaction.

Simultaneously with the assessment of changes in present morbidity, the costs incurred by the community in terms of lost production were estimated. Approximate estimates of the costs incurred directly by the hospital in treating the patients could be derived from the hospital costing returns. Hence the cost study concentrated on the value to society of the production lost by each patient, his relatives and friends, while the patient was being treated at the hospital. To our knowledge a study of this size and detail (covering 1,600 patients) has not been done previously. The distinctive features of the method were the following: the whole community including the patient was treated as the unit which incurred costs, and the loss of both unpaid and paid production was estimated in detail. A description of this cost study can be obtained from the authors.

The classification described here was developed and used to measure the Sanative Output of St. Olave's Hospital in a study lasting one month, immediately prior to the organizational change. It is shown in the form used in the study in Figure 9.1 and a brief reminder to the clinician, included on the back of the form as in Figure 9.2, provides a summary of the more important features.

There are eight classes of disability and four of distress, giving a total of thirty-two possible classes, one of which is absence of disability and distress, although this need not correspond to perfect health. This form does not include death since this is routinely recorded by the hospital. The categories of disability are fairly discrete, but in a case of doubt between two categories the clinician was asked to choose the worse one. In practice this was rarely necessary. There are only four categories of distress owing to the difficulty in resolving this further using clinical judgment only.

Medical treatment may involve trading between states. Some degree of disability is frequently accepted in exchange for relief of pain or depression, and this becomes apparent in the changing states of patients recorded during hospital treatment.

This taxonomy distinguishes between the observable state of the patient's disability and his subjective feelings or distress. This initial division has been found to be particularly useful both for the assessment of patients and for scaling, but further dimensions could be introduced. Both disability and distress could be further sub-divided as illustrated for example by the notes on definitions of distress included in Figure 9.2.

FIGURE 9.1

Part II   (To be completed by clinican seeing patient).

Please tick the appropriate disability and distress state for this patient.
Please consult the instructions on the back of this form if you are not familiar with them.

Your name...

Col. 12 *Disability*.
 ☐ 1 No disability.
 ☐ 2 Slight social disability.
 ☐ 3 Severe social disability and/or slight impairment of performance at work. Able to do all housework except very heavy tasks.
 ☐ 4 Choice of work or performance at work severely limited.
       Housewives and old people able to do light housework only, but able to go out shopping.
 ☐ 5 Unable to undertake any paid employment. Unable to continue any education. Old people confined to home except for escorted outings and short walks and unable to do shopping. Housewives only able to perform a few simple tasks.
 ☐ 6 Confined to chair or to wheelchair or able to move around in the home only with support from an assistant.
 ☐ 7 Confined to bed.
 ☐ 8 Unconscious.

Col. 13 *Distress*.
 ☐ 1 No distress.
 ☐ 2 Mild.
 ☐ 3 Moderate.
 ☐ 4 Severe.

Col. 14 *For Outpatients Only*.
If the patient is being discharged from the clinic today please tick this box ☐ (1).

FIGURE 9.2

NOTES ON DEFINITIONS OF DISABILITY
This describes the extent to which a patient is unable to pursue the activities of a normal person at the time at which the classification is made. If you are uncertain in choosing between two categories, choose the lower one.
Patients in Class 2 are slightly disabled, but performance in their normal work is not impaired. This degree of disablement may affect social activities and personal relationships. It includes such conditions as mild cosmetic defects, slight injuries and diseases which may interfere with hobbies but not with essential activities, and some of the less severe psychiatric states which cause some social disablement.

NOTES ON DEFINITIONS OF DISTRESS
This describes patients' pain, mental suffering in relation to disablement, anxiety and depression.
    i.e.   Pain and/or mental disturbance and/or reaction to disability.

PAIN
    State 1.   None.
    State 2.   The patient has mild pain such as that of mild toothache for which analgesics such as aspirin might be prescribed.
    State 3.   The patient has moderate pain e.g. severe migraine-type headache.
    State 4.   The patient has severe pain e.g. due to subarachnoid haemorrhage. Pains for which morphine might be prescribed.

MENTAL DISTURBANCE
    State 1.   No mental disturbance.
    State 2.   Mild mental distress.
    State 3.   Moderate mental distress.
    State 4.   Severe mental distress.

REACTION TO DISABILITY
Patients who are distressed in reaction to disability will normally be classed in distress state 2 if they are in disability state 5 or 6—distress state 3 if they are disability state 7 but there will clearly be individual variations in the extent of their acceptance of disability.

The morbidity classification, to be useful in practice, must satisfy the following criteria:

1. It must be used reliably by the same clinicians on different occasions. (Test—retest reliability.)
2. It must be used reliably by different clinicians.
3. Reliability must be obtained between different specialities. (Inter-observer reliability.)
4. It must be acceptable to staff. It must therefore be quick to apply and a high level of co-operation must be obtained.

As the number of categories is increased, it becomes more difficult to satisfy these criteria, but as the number is reduced, the sensitivity of the measure is likely to diminish. The classification described here has been developed through a series of pilot studies and a reasonable level of performance has been obtained as measured against these criteria. although there is room for improvement, given a more leisurely experimental situation.

The level of agreement in the use of the form by clinicians improves rapidly with practice, and with not more than one training session it was possible to achieve, with groups of 3 or 4 clinicians, a Kendall Coefficient of Concordance which averaged 0.9. Some groups achieved this at the first attempt.

During the study the form was used by 48 doctors at St. Olave's on 2,120 patients. During the month under study 16 changes of medical staff occurred. This turnover-rate is not unusual. This reduced the level of repeatability attained in practice as it was not always possible to train these people adequately. Once the staff became experienced the classification took about ten seconds. This is important because the sensitivity of the measure may be increased by more frequent estimates of morbidity, for example, daily assessment, although the choice of the optimal interval raises a number of theoretical problems [9].

During the month of the study the classifications satisfied the criteria described above to the following extent:

1. Repeatable by same doctor   92%
2. Repeatable by different doctors   83%
3. Consistent across specialities   90%

4. Acceptable to staff
   —co-operation   98%
   —low omission rate   3%
   —quick   10 seconds

Results

The disability and distress states of in-patients on admission for the month of the study are shown in Figure 3. On admission the patients were well spread over the disability and distress states, although in this period no patients were admitted in an unconscious state. Nineteen per cent of the patients were admitted in

FIGURE 9.3. **Percentage of patients in each morbidity state on admission**

Distress state / Disability state	1	2	3	4
1	19	12	3	1
2	10	12	3	1
3	1	3	1	1
4	3	3	5	1
5	1	3	4	2
6	1	1	2	0
7	1	2	3	1
8	0	0	0	0

morbidity state (*1, 1*), i.e. with no disability and distress. They were presumably admitted for action on their prognosis, which is not covered by the study described here.

On discharge (Figure 9.4), the number of patients falling into this category had increased to 33%. In general there was a move towards the top left-hand corner of the matrix. This trend continued until the first out-patient visit (see Figure 9.5).

These matrices provide a summary of the changes occurring in the patients' disability and distress during the episode of hospital care. However, the matrices are too complex for rapid comprehensive and manipulation. In comparing them, it is necessary to make valuations of the relative benefits of the transition from each state to any other state.

FIGURE 9.4   **Percentage of patients in each morbidity state at discharge**

	1	2	3	4
1	33	10	1	0
2	21	11	1	0
3	2	3	1	0
4	3	4	1	0
5	3	2	2	1
6	0	0	1	0
7	0	0	0	0
8	0	0	0	0

FIGURE 9.5   **Percentage of patients in each morbidity state at first out-patient attendance after discharge**

	1	2	3	4
1	45	7	0	0
2	7	11	2	0
3	3	4	2	0
4	1	2	2	0
5	2	8	1	0
6	1	1	1	0
7	0	0	0	0
8	0	0	0	0

Suppose a scale could be developed which stated that discharging a patient in state $(1, 1)$ after admission in $(7, 4)$ was worth x points and after admission in $(5, 2)$ was worth y points. Also suppose the scale had the property that discharging a patient in $(5, 2)$ after admission in $(7, 4)$ was worth $(x-y)$ points. Such a scale could then be used to weight the various changes which occurred so that the effect of the hospital on the immediate health of its patients, the Sanative Output, would be expressed by the number of scalar points. This simple measure could be used in the comparison of the concurrent achievements of different health services or of one service over time. The next section discusses the methods by which such a scale might be developed and describes the derivation of a scale from the awards made by the courts in personal injury cases.

The development of a scale to weight the relative importance of the defined symptom states

We have taken the view that for the purpose of resource allocation a ratio scale is highly desirable and hence we have explored ways of deriving a ratio scale for the defined morbidity states. Interval scales have been used in the USA for general disability and for improvement in mental health [6; 10] and recently in England [4].

There are two main approaches used to derive ratio scales for entities such as symptom states. A scale could be obtained from survey data collected using carefully structured questionnaires and/or interviews. Alternatively a behavioural method could be used on the assumption that social behaviour involves implicit weighting of the transitions between states, and that if the appropriate social variables can be identified it should be possible to make this implicit scale explicit.

The opinion survey approach permits control of the value judgment situation and specification of the data required. It suffers from the disadvantage that what people say they do and what they actually do may be very different. The behavioural approach does not have this disadvantage. However, the situations studied are not under the observer's control and the data is usually sketchy.

These are general problems, but there are also major difficulties involved in the details of the available methods using either of these approaches. The two approaches appear to complement one another. Agreement between them could provide some indication of the validity of the results. We are therefore adopting both approaches. Using the empirically derived classification described in this paper, more progress has been made with the behavioural approach. However, we anticipate that extensive re-evaluation of this and other methods will be necessary and this may in turn involve modifications of the symptom states used.

The particular behaviour which has been studied is the award of compensation by the courts to the victims of injury and disease. The aim of these awards may be interpreted as the neutralization of the disability and distress suffered by the plaintiff. Reports of the cases heard in the high courts and courts of appeal frequently contain detailed information on the plaintiff's clinical state and they separate, from the total award, the non-pecuniary element awarded entirely as compensation for injury and illness. Judges have frequently commented on the emergence of a scale of awards which is related solely to the relative severities of different degrees of disability and distress. The problems and advantages of this method and the details of the method of analysis are discussed at length elsewhere [8].

Using the accounts of the court case, the plaintiff's disability and distress were assessed. Clinicians, given summaries of a patient's case notes describing the patient's state at a particular time, were found to make the same assessment of the patient's state as they did when seeing the patient in hospital at that time. A group of doctors, given summaries based on records of court cases together with summaries of case notes, made consistent assessments of disability and distress and did not discriminate between the two types of record. There is thus some evidence to support this method of handling court case reports.

An analysis of about five hundred awards has produced the provisional scale shown in Figure 9.6. The series of computer analyses has taken into account the effects of inflation and of the life expectancy of the plaintiff. Since it is the ratios between the various states which are of interest, a value of unity has been assigned to the lowest states and the other values derived by dividing the mean award for each state by the mean award for the lowest state.

Suitable legal cases have been found to cover most of the categories of disability and distress. Ninety-seven per cent of the classifications made during the study are covered by this scale. However, there are certain disability/distress states where it is unlikely that court awards will ever be available in any number, for example, 5–1, 6–1, 7–1, which are categories with a high level of disability without distress. The presumption of the courts is that the sick person must suffer distress, whilst the observation of doctors is that they do not always do so, particularly after a period of adjustment to chronic disability.

The numbers of cases for which full details were available are shown in Figure 9.7 and the coefficients of variation for those classes containing more than five cases are shown in Figure 9.8.

Using this provisional scale the Sanative Output (this is the

Analysis of awards made for General Damages

Figure 9.6			Provisional Scale		
	Distress	*1*	*2*	*3*	*4*
Disability					
1		0·0	1·0	1·9	—
2		2·1	3·0	5·1	8·3
3		4·4	6·5	14·0	30·0
4		16·0	16·0	31·0	38·0
5		52·0	52·0	59·0	66·0
6		—	59·0	66·0	121·0
7		—	—	114·0	158·0
8		123·0	—	—	—

Figure 9.7			Sample Size		
	Distress	*1*	*2*	*3*	*4*
Disability					
1		—	12·0	2·0	—
2		9·0	25·0	9·0	1·0
3		12·0	40·0	29·0	2·0
4		17·0	41·0	58·0	21·0
5		1·0	13·0	17·0	6·0
6		—	2·0	4·0	15·0
7		—	—	2·0	7·0
8		5·0	—	—	—

Figure 9.8			Coefficients of Variation		
	Distress	*1*	*2*	*3*	*4*
Disability					
1		—	0·33	—	—
2		0·23	0·40	0·36	—
3		0·53	0·43	0·43	—
4		0·53	0·43	0·57	0·59
5		—	0·43	0·56	0·38
6		—	0·56	0·58	0·50
7		—	—	—	0·62
8		0·33	—	—	—

scaled changes in the immediate symptoms of the patients treated) of St Olave's during the month studied was 3,800 units.

It is interesting to compare the Sanative Output with the maximum change in immediate health which could be produced by a perfect system, that is one which discharged all its patients with neither disability nor distress. This we call the Sanative Potential of the system.

St Olave's achieved 30% of the Sanative Potential in the period of one month.

Conclusions

These figures for Sanative Output and Sanative Potential are of course meaningless in isolation. It is the possibility of seeing how they change over time at St Olave's and of comparing St Olave's with other hospitals which makes them potentially valuable. In particular, since the operational definition adopted for Sanative Output compares the morbidity state of the untreated patient on entry to the hospital with his treated state later in the episode of care, it does not distinguish between those changes which are a result of treatment and those which result from the natural progress of the disease. This will complicate comparisons between hospitals which have very different case mixes.

Sanative Output and Sanative Potential have been chosen as measures of performance as we have found them to be readily understood. Their use to monitor performance should help to focus attention on those areas where improvements in performance are most likely to be obtained. However, investigation of such areas would probably draw, where appropriate, on the more detailed descriptions of symptoms and signs used by clinicians. Another way of expressing the results would be in the form of the probability of transition from each state to every other state. A comparison of the transition matrices obtained from different hospitals or from the same hospital at different times would enable some of the effects of case mix variations to be eliminated.

The use of legal awards has permitted a scale to be developed for the defined morbidity states. There is no compelling reason why the judgments about morbidity states made by judges sitting in the high court and court of appeal should be the most appropriate judgments to use to assess the performance of a hospital. Other judgments should be sought to identify any major difference of opinion which might exist. The development of alternative scaling procedures which would make possible the comparison of this scale based on legal awards with scales based on the judgments of other individuals or groups of individuals is of high priority. The detailed analysis required by such scaling procedures of the way in which individuals view different morbidity states may in turn affect the choice of the classification.

References

1. Bispham, K., Stringer, J. and Holland, W. W., 'Planning for Health', *The Hospital*, pp. 1–6, March 1971

2. Cochrane, A. L., 'Effectiveness and Efficiency', Rock Carling Fellowship, Nuffield Provincial Hospitals Trust, p. 77, 1971

3. Fanshel, S. and Bush, J., 'A Health Status Index and its Application to Health Services Outcomes', Operations Research October–December, p. 1021, 1971

4. Grogono, A. W. and Woodgate, D. J., 'Index for measuring health', *Lancet* ii, 1024, 1971

5. Logan, R. F. L., Klein, R. E. and Ashley, J. S. A., 'Effective Management of Health', *British Medical Journal*, 2, 519, 1971

6. Mahoney, F. I. and Barthel, D. W., 'Functional Evaluation', The Barthel Index, *Maryland Medical Journal*, 14, 61, 1965

7. Rosser, R. M. and Watts, V. C., 'The Measurement of Hospital Output', *International Journal of Epidemiology*, 4, 1972

8. Rosser, R. M. and Watts, V. C., 'The use of classification of morbidity to analyse the consistency of the awards made by the Courts in personal injury cases'. Part of discussion paper presented to the SSRC conference on the Cost of Human Impairment, March 1973. Copies available from the authors

9. Sullivan, D. F., 'Conceptual Problems in Developing an Index of Health', Office of Health Statistics Analysis, Department of Health Education and Welfare, Washington, 1966

10. Wartsk, S. A. and Green, D. S., 'Evaluation in a Home Care Program', *Medical Care*, 9, 352, 1971

Conclusion

It is not possible to go into the details of precise topics or appropriate methodologies for future research in the areas discussed in this book. However it is interesting to note some of the general aspects that seem open to further investigation.

We need to know a lot more about the incentive/disincentive effects of different measures on behaviour, particularly risk-taking behaviour. Road accidents are the obvious example of instances where quite extraordinary risks continue to be taken in the face of well-publicised advice on their probable outcome. The questions to be answered cover a wide range, particularly at the level of individual and group motivations to modify risk-taking behaviour. Present advertising campaigns on both wearing seat belts and stopping smoking suggest that appeals to vanity may be more effective than straightforward appeals for prudence, but this is founded on hunches rather than advances in the psychology of motivation.

Another approach to the problem of finding the right incentive to change behaviour might be through the pocket, by imposing on certain groups the brunt of costs of accident avoidance. For example, under-25's might be required to pay for a large portion of road safety measures since they are the age-group with the highest accident rate. Work needs to be done too on the responsiveness of motorists to changes in insurance premiums.

At the other end of the spectrum, we need research into the individual disabled people and their immediate families. The most obvious fields here for exploration are those concerned with the minimization of the costs of disability once it has been incurred and the maximization of independence for the disabled. These considerations might be complementary or conflicting, for obvious reasons; what is required is elucidation of the alternatives and their relative costs, in the fullest sense of that word. We also need to know how compensation both by state and through the law courts is viewed by the client. An important bone of current contention is whether compensation payments should necessarily be paid in a lump sum (the courts) or by periodic payments (state benefits) or in kind (training for re-remployment support services) and contributions towards elucidating an answer could be made through finding out how individuals have actually fared under the different parts of the system, and how they themselves perceive and value the various mechanisms for compensation.

We also need to find out a great deal more about the impact of disability on the family. Little is known at present about the household as a producing, consuming and caring unit, or the consequences of misfortune for this unit, and information on this is clearly essential for any real attempt to evaluate alternative care systems for disabled people.

At the administrative level, there are gaps in our knowledge of official behaviour and even of the relative merits and defects of different systems of health care. Thus, the attitudes of administrators and officials all too often exhibit the reverse side of the risk-taking coin: that is to say, they have a strong tendency to avoid risk-taking in decision-making, and to stick to well-known formulae as a basis for allocating resources. We need studies of the prevalence of these attitudes, of their causes and their effect on decisions, and of possible ways of mitigating them and encouraging officialdom to be more open-minded and perhaps less cautious in its approach. Such studies could either be seen as part of a comprehensive review of comparative systems of care, or as part of a general study of decision-making at intermediate levels.

Finally, we need to know more about the very delicate and difficult issues of our social values and ethics. It is well known that there are ever-increasing numbers of 'survivors' among the various groups of disabled; the congenitally disabled who no longer die within the first few years of birth: the survivors (but only just) of severe road accidents; and, numerically the most important, the old people with chronic and disabling conditions. At the moment the prevailing ethic appears to be the preservation and maintenance of life, even at minimal level, at all costs. Yet behind this is a ground swell of contrary opinion, particularly from those in close daily contact with severely disabled people such as doctors, nurses and relatives, which suggests that the costs—psychological and emotional as much as economic—of maintaining some of these lives are too great to bear.

Allied to this are ethical problems connected with possible reduction in the incidence of congenital disability, through active preventive measures before and after conception. Whilst genetic counselling itself is generally ethically acceptable, its implications in terms of possible sterilization, abortion and, eventually, of genetic engineering have raised considerable controversy. We have, however, little reliable evidence of how far this is a true reflection of general attitudes and feelings.

Appendix A

Impaired and Handicapped People — a few facts and figures

This Appendix does not purport to do other than to give a few basic facts and figures on impaired and handicapped people, and the benefits and services available to them. The major source of information has been the Government Survey[1] which was carried out in late 1968 and early 1969 (the OPCS Survey) but other sources have also been drawn on. Further information can be obtained from the official publications, some of which are named at the end of this Appendix, of the Department of Health and Social Security, the Department of Employment and other Departments whose responsibilities touch on the needs of impaired and handicapped people. Since these sources use different definitions of such terms as 'impaired', 'handicapped', etc.—bodies compiling statistics naturally use definitions that accord with their own purposes—the terms used throughout this Appendix are not necessarily consistent.

The OPCS Survey defined 'impairment' as 'lacking part or all of a limb, or having a defective limb, organ or mechanism of the body'; 'disablement' as 'the loss or reduction of functional ability'; and 'handicap' as 'the disadvantage or restriction of activity caused by disability'.

The OPCS Survey was confined to adults living at home in Great Britain and therefore omitted, for example, hospital in-patients and children. But these are not the only gaps in information on this subject. For example, it is not possible to provide any sort of precise estimate of the total resources involved in the services available to the handicapped. Certain services are specific to them and where this is the case the information on costs and expenditure is unambiguous. In other categories, however, the handicapped share common services with others (e.g. the elderly) and such categories of expenditure do not lend themselves to disaggregation between the handicapped and other groups.

---

[1] 'Handicapped and Impaired in Great Britain'. Office of Population Censuses and Surveys. Parts I and II (1971) and Part III (1972). HMSO. £3.25, £2.85 and £0.85 respectively.

Finally, some selection of what information to provide as background material is inevitable; the following aims to provide an indication of the size of the problems involved and the services and facilities available.

Section I deals with the size of the impaired and handicapped population analysed in different ways. Section II indicates what benefits are available by way of cash, while Section III shows what services are available to assist with health, welfare and employment problems.

SECTION I

THE SIZE OF THE IMPAIRED AND HANDICAPPED POPULATION

The OPCS Survey was based on a representative sample of 250,000 households and covered people of 16 years of age or over living at home in Great Britain, chiefly with regard to their ability to perform certain specified activities of daily living. Certain groups such as the blind, the deaf, the mentally ill and the mentally handicapped, people with diabetes and people with epilepsy, were included only if their impairment limited in some way their mobility or their ability to work or care for themselves. People in residential homes, hospitals, etc. were also excluded, as were children.

The OPCS Survey found that there were about 1·1 million people in the Survey's first 6 Categories, i.e. 'very severely', 'severely' and 'appreciably' handicapped (the remaining categories, 7 and 8, had minor or no handicaps). Taking these findings into account and adding very broad estimates for those not covered by the Survey, the total number of very severely, severely and appreciably handicapped people of all ages in Great Britain might be of the order of 1½ million.[1]

Total numbers of impaired people, by age group

Table A.1 indicates that over 3 million people aged 16 or over living in private households in Great Britain could be considered to be impaired within the OPCS Survey definition; of them 1¼ million were male and over 1¾ million female. The majority (over 1¾ million) of the impaired were over 65. ('Impairment' covered, of course, all 8 categories of the OPCS Survey.)

---

[1] Hansard (Commons) 19 November 1973. Vol. 864, No. 15.

TABLE A.1 **Estimated numbers of men and women
in different age groups, living in private households,
who had some impairment**

GREAT BRITAIN

| Age Group | Estimated Numbers | | |
	Men	Women	Men and Women
16–29	50,000	39,000	89,000
30–49	197,000	170,000	366,000
50–64	401,000	433,000	833,000
65–74	356,000	559,000	915,000
75 and over	243,000	625,000	867,000
All ages	1,247,000	1,825,000	3,071,000

Table 2 shows that approximately 1 in 13 people aged 16 or over
living in private households had some physical, mental or sensory
impairment, the figures for men and women separately being about
1 in 15 and 1 in 11 respectively. As age increased so did the incidence
of impairment, for the over 75's rising to over 3 in 10 for men and
over 4 in 10 for women.

TABLE A.2 **Proportion per 1,000 of men and women in different
age groups, in private households, with some impairment**

GREAT BRITAIN

| Age Group | Proportion per 1,000 with Impairment | | |
	Men	Women	Men and Women
16–29	10·0	7·9	8·9
30–49	30·2	25·6	27·9
50–64	85·6	84·6	85·0
65–74	211·4	227·1	220·7
75 and over	316·2	409·0	378·0
All ages	66·7	88·2	78·0

Degrees of handicap, by sex and age group
On the question of the numbers of impaired people with varying
degrees of handicap and living in private households, the OPCS
Survey suggests that there were about 25,000 (5,000 men and 20,000
I.D.H.—7*

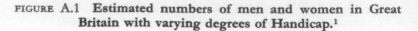

FIGURE A.1   **Estimated numbers of men and women in Great Britain with varying degrees of Handicap.**[1]

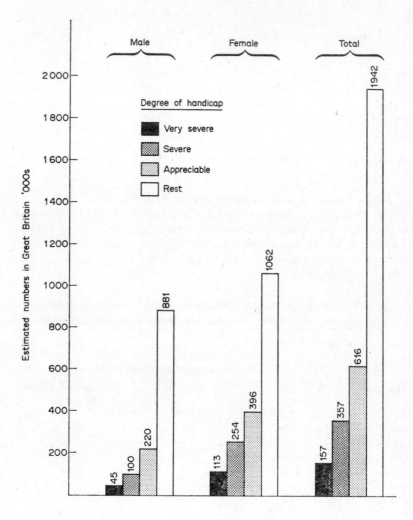

[1] Based on the OPCS Survey, which excluded certain groups, e.g. people in hospitals and residential homes: see page 173 above.

FIGURE A.2 **Degree of handicap of impaired people in different age groups and estimated numbers in Great Britain.**[1]

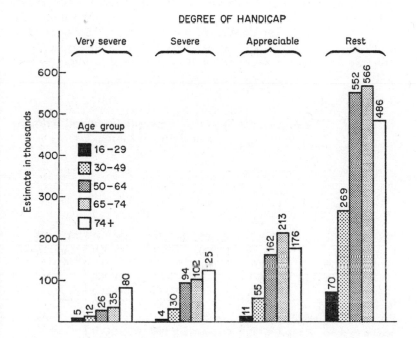

[1] Based on the OPCS Survey, which excluded certain groups, e.g. people in hospitals and residential homes: see page 173 above.

women) in the groups covered by the Survey who were so severely handicapped as to require a good deal of care or supervision every day and practically every night. In addition there were about 133,000 needing constant day care.

Figure A.1 indicates the distribution of severity of handicap for males and females. Broadly speaking, 'very severely' handicapped is defined as 'needing special care', 'severely' handicapped as 'needing considerable support', 'appreciably' handicapped as 'needing some support' and the rest as 'impaired, but needing little or no support for normal everyday living activities'.

Incidence of severity, as might be expected, varies by age, so that of those very severely handicapped (157,000), 116,000 (of whom 90,000 are women) were 65 or over, about two-thirds of whom were at least 75 years old. At the other end of the age scale, there were 3,000 men and 2,000 women under 30 who were very severely handicapped.

Figure A.2 indicates the distribution of severity of handicap by age.

TABLE A.3 **Working status of impaired people (men and women) of working age, and living at home.**

GREAT BRITAIN

Age	16–29	30–49	*50–64*	*Totals*	
Working	43,000	185,000	265,000	493,000	635,000† (employment field)
Unemployed	8,000	17,000	24,000	49,000	
Temporarily sick	4,000	32,000	56,000	93,000	
Occupational Centre	7,000	4,000	—	11,000	
Housewife*	7,000	61,000	203,000	271,000	637,000 (at home)
Retired	—	—	78,000	78,000	
Permanently disabled, unable to work again	17,000	66,000	205,000	291,000	
Totals	89,000	366,000	833,000	1,288,000	

Note:

* 'Housewife' is defined here as a person who is not part of the labour force and not seeking employment. It should be noted that this differs from the definition used elsewhere in the OPCS Survey report.

† The Department of Employment Discussion Paper Resettlement Policy and Services for Disabled People (1972) suggests that there may be altogether one million impaired people at work.

Employment and impairment
The OPCS Survey indicated that the impaired population of working age (i.e. 16–64) was split more or less evenly between those in employment and those at home. About half those unemployed and over 70% of those 'permanently disabled, unable to work again' were in the age group 50–64.

TABLE A.4   **Main cause of impairment**

GREAT BRITAIN

| | Estimated numbers living at home | | |
	Men and Women	Men	Women
Diseases of bones and organs of movement	1,187,000	351,000	836,000
Diseases of circulatory system	492,000	199,000	292,000
Diseases of central nervous system	360,000	163,000	197,000
Diseases of respiratory system	284,000	179,000	104,000
Disorders of sense organs (including blindness)	277,000	92,000	186,000
Amputations	129,000	105,000	24,000
Senility and ill defined conditions	122,000	40,000	82,000
Injuries	114,000	73,000	41,000
Mental, psycho-neurotic and personality disorders	98,000	38,000	60,000
Diseases of digestive system	82,000	35,000	47,000
Allergic, endocrine, metabolic and nutritional diseases	51,000	16,000	35,000
Diseases of genito-urinary system	35,000	9,200	26,000
Infective and parasitic diseases	30,000	17,000	12,000
Diseases of blood and blood-forming organs	28,000	4,100	24,000
Neoplasms	27,000	13,000	15,000
Diseases of skin and cellular tissue	20,000	9,400	11,000
Congenital malformations	16,000	5,500	10,000
Totals	3,352,000	1,349,200	2,002,000

Of the labour force excluding 'housewives' and retired persons, 55% were working, 1% attending an occupation centre, 5% unemployed, 9% off sick temporarily and 30% permanently disabled and unable to work again. As might be expected, the proportion working falls and the proportion permanently disabled and unable to work again rises as the severity of handicap increases, being 6% and 85% respectively for the very severely handicapped.

Causes of impairment and of incapacity for work

Tables A.4, A.5 and A.6 provide background information on impairment and incapacity for work, by cause. Table A.4, based on the OPCS Survey, identifies the number of impaired people (among those covered by the Survey) by main cause of impairment. Disease of bones and organs of movement (largely arthritis) contributed a substantial proportion of the total (35%), particularly for impaired women (42%).

Tables A.5(i) and A.5(ii) show that certain forms of impairment were more handicapping than others, with multiple sclerosis topping the table. (Based on the OPCS Survey of adults living at home.)

Table A.6 is taken from social security statistics relating to duration of spells of incapacity for sickness and invalidity benefits and provides an indication of which diseases are more incapacitating (in terms of duration) than others.

TABLE A.5(i)		TABLE A.5(ii)	
GREAT BRITAIN			
Illnesses and Conditions with highest proportion of very severely/severely handicapped (in percentages)		Illnesses and Conditions with lowest proportion of very severely/severely handicapped (in percentages)	
Condition	*Ppn suffering who are very severely/ severely handicapped*	*Condition*	*Ppn suffering who are very severely/ severely handicapped*
Multiple sclerosis	65	Sciatica	2
Parkinson's disease	52	Skin and cellular	
Strokes	52	tissue diseases	6
Paraplegia/		Epilepsy	10
hemiplegia	34		
Spastic	24		
Arthritis	20		

TABLE A.6 **Spells of certified incapacity terminating in the period 7.6.71 to 3.6.72. Analysis by cause of incapacity and duration (sickness and invalidity benefits).**

GREAT BRITAIN

Cause of Incapacity	All Durations	1–24 Thousands	%	25–156 Thousands	%	157–312 Thousands	%	Over 312 Thousands	%
All causes	8,394	6,623	79	1,587	19	91	1	94	1
All causes except influenza	7,455	5,735	77	1,537	21	90	1	94	1
Infective and parasitic diseases	705	643	91	57	8	2	—	3	—
Tuberculosis of respiratory system	6	1	12	2	41	1	18	2	29
Neoplasms	23	13	55	8	35	1	5	1	5
Endocrine, nutritional and metabolic diseases	38	20	54	14	37	1	4	2	
Diseases of blood and blood forming organs	35	25	72	9	24	1	2	1	2
Mental disorders	280	175	63	87	31	8	3	9	3
Diseases of nervous system and sense organs	238	170	71	57	24	5	2	7	3
Disease of circulatory system	265	106	40	121	46	15	6	23	9
Hypertensive diseases	48	20	42	21	45	2	5	4	8
Ischaemic heart disease	76	16	21	44	58	6	9	10	13
Diseases of respiratory system	3,091	2,784	90	278	9	11	—	18	1
Influenza	939	888	95	50	5	—	—	—	—
Bronchitis excluding acute bronchitis	603	456	76	126	21	8	1	13	2
Diseases of digestive system	628	445	71	172	27	7	1	4	1
Diseases of genito-urinary system	220	168	77	48	22	3	1	1	1
Diseases of pregnancy, childbirth and puerperium	126	32	26	93	74	1	1	—	—
Diseases of skin and subcutaneous tissue	238	195	82	40	17	1	1	1	—
Diseases of musculoskeletal system and connective tissue	680	482	71	176	26	12	2	11	2
Arthritis and rheumatism except rheumatic fever	404	297	74	93	23	6	2	8	2
Congenital anomalies	3	2	54	1	33	—	3	—	11
Symptoms and ill-defined conditions	851	622	73	210	25	12	1	6	1
Accidents, poisonings and violence	973	739	76	217	22	11	1	6	1

SECTION II
CASH BENEFITS FOR WHICH IMPAIRED AND HANDICAPPED PEOPLE MAY QUALIFY

Sickness and Invalidity Benefits

In common with the rest of the insured population, impaired and handicapped people may qualify for sickness benefit, followed by invalidity benefit, if they are incapable of work. (Some may not qualify because they have never worked and paid the necessary national insurance contributions.)

Main Rates from October 1973[1]		Per week £
First two weeks (Sickness benefit)	Personal	7.35
	Wife or other dependant	4.55
	Children:	
	First child	2.30
	Second child	1.40
	Each other child	1.30
Next 26 weeks	Additional earnings related supplement up to	7.00
		(£8.47 from 7 January 1974)
After 28 weeks (Invalidity pension)	Personal	7.55
	Wife or other adult dependant	4.75
	Children:	
	First child	3.80
	Second child	2.90
	Each other child	2.80
	Invalidity allowance (additional)	
	Becoming incapable of work:	
	Before the age of 35	1.60
	Between age 35 and under 45	1.00
	Between age 45 and under 60 men / 55 women	0.50

[1] The rates of cash benefits are now reviewed every year. Where there is title to family allowances, they continue, of course, to be paid during periods for which benefits are payable.

In 1972 there were 9·8 million new claims for sickness benefit in Great Britain and during the year about 200,000 people became eligible for invalidity pensions. At any one time there are about 400,000 invalidity pensioners, more than three-quarters of whom also receive invalidity allowances (at 31 May 1972, the figures were 415,000 and 82% respectively).

In 1972–73 sickness benefit cost £295 million and invalidity benefit cost £196 million. At the benefit rates introduced in October 1973, the annual cost of sickness benefit could be of the order of £380 million and the annual cost of invalidity benefit could be of the order of £230 million.

Unemployment Benefit

Individuals who lose their jobs may be eligible for unemployment benefit. Impaired and handicapped people must satisfy the ordinary conditions, including being capable of, and available for work. The rates are the same as the rates of sickness benefit.

Attendance allowance

Attendance allowance is payable at two rates. To qualify for the higher rate—£6.20 a week from October 1973—a person must be so handicapped physically or mentally that for six months or more he has required a great deal of help from another person both by day *and* at night. The lower rate—£4.15 a week from October 1973—is payable where the condition is satisfied either by day *or* at night. Allowances at these rates can also be paid, from age 2, for handicapped children who satisfy an additional condition that the attention or supervision they require is substantially in excess of that normally required by a child of the same age and sex. In September 1973, the higher rate attendance allowance was being paid to 97,000 people in Great Britain at an annual cost of over £31 million.

Supplementary benefit

Supplementary benefit is normally payable only to people who are not in full-time work but it can be paid to a handicapped self-employed person whose earning power is substantially reduced compared with others in the same occupation. The benefit paid is normally the amount by which a person's 'requirements' exceed his 'resources'. Where a handicapped person is able to do only part-time work, the first £2 a week of his earnings are normally disregarded.

The scales provided from October 1973 for normal day-to-day living expenses are:

	Ordinary Weekly Rates	Long-term Weekly Rates Claimant (and Wife) under 80	Claimant or Wife aged 80 or over
	£	£	£
Married couple	11.65	12.85	13.10
Single householder	7.15	8.15	8.40
Any other person aged 18 or over	5.70	6.60	6.85
Any other person aged 16 to 17	4.40		
Dependent children aged up to 15 (by age of child)	2.05– 3.70		

Special rates apply for blind people.

The long-term scales apply to those—except the unemployed—who have been receiving supplementary benefit for a continuous period of two years (and to all people over pensionable age).

An allowance for rent is added to these amounts. For a householder, this is normally, in the case of rented accommodation, the total rent and rates paid; for owner occupied accommodation, it is made up of rates, mortgage interest, ground rent or feu duty and an allowance for repairs and insurance. For people living in someone else's household, a standard rent addition of 80p is made.

An addition can sometimes be made to help meet the cost of special expenses such as extra heating, domestic help, or special diets.

Those people who are entitled to attendance allowance have the amount of that allowance added to their requirements.

In November 1972, 136,000 people classified in supplementary benefit statistics as 'sick and disabled' in Great Britain were receiving both supplementary benefit and national insurance benefit. In addition, 164,000 'sick and disabled' people were receiving the former but not the latter. The cost of supplementary benefit paid to people of working age who are incapable of work is estimated at over £80 million a year.

People receiving supplementary benefit and their dependants are automatically entitled to free prescriptions, dental treatment, dentures and glasses, as well as free milk and vitamins for children under school age and expectant mothers, and free school meals for school children. People not eligible for supplementary benefit may also be able to get help, even if they are in full-time work, if their income is below a certain level.

Injury Benefit

Injury benefit is payable for six months to those incapable of work as a result of an industrial accident or a prescribed industrial disease. Beyond this period, injury benefit ceases but sickness benefit or invalidity benefit may be payable as well as any entitlement to disablement pension (see below).

The rate of injury benefit from October 1973 is £10.10 a week. Increases are payable for dependants at the same rates as in the case of sickness benefit.

In 1972, there were 700,000 new claims for injury benefit in Great Britain. The cost of the benefit in 1972–73 was £32 million. At current rates, it could cost about £40 million a year.

Disablement Benefits—Industrial Injuries and War Pensions Schemes

Entitlement to these disablement benefit is based upon 'loss of faculty'

—i.e. any pathological condition or any loss (including a reduction) of the normal physical or mental function of some organ or part of the body—caused by the relevant injury. The rate of benefit is dependent on the extent and likely duration of the disability resulting from such loss of faculty. For assessments of 20% and upwards the benefit is a weekly pension, and for 1% to 19% assessments the benefit is normally a lump sum. Both schemes provide allowances for unemployability, the need for constant attendance and exceptionally severe disablement. Certain other allowances are also payable—e.g. with War Pensions for age, wear and tear of clothing, etc.

	Per week
Basic Rates from October 1973	£
100% disablement	12.80
Maximum additional payment for loss of earning power	5.12
Unemployability supplement	
(*a*) Industrial Injuries Scheme	7.75
(*b*) War Pensions Scheme	8.40
Constant attendance allowance	5.15–10.30

At the end of September 1973, 347,000 war disablement pensions were being paid. Together with associated allowances, the total cost of such pensions was £99 million in 1972–73. At current (October 1973) rates, the cost could be of the order of £112 million a year.

At the end of September 1972, there were 204,000 industrial disablement pensions in payment. Industrial disablement pensions cost £78 million in 1972–73. At current (October 1973) rates, the cost could be about £97 million a year.

Grants, etc. for families of handicapped children

The Government has set up 'The Family Fund' to help, by way of goods, services or grants, families with children who are very severely handicapped from birth. It is administered independently by the Rowntree Memorial Trust.[1]

Family income supplement

Family income supplement helps low-income families with one or more children where the breadwinner is in full-time work. 'Full-time' work means 30 or more hours' work a week (so bringing in the handicapped worker whose working week is restricted to that extent).

---

[1] The Family Fund, Joseph Rowntree Memorial Trust, Beverley House, Shipton Road, York, Y03, 6RB.

SECTION III
SERVICES AVAILABLE TO IMPAIRED
AND HANDICAPPED PEOPLE

Central government and local authorities provide a number of services for impaired and handicapped people. Frequently the services are not specific to these people and it is not always possible to identify separately how much of a particular service is directed to, or used by them.

Hospital services

Rehabilitation services, i.e. physiotherapy, including hydrotherapy, occupational therapy and remedial exercises are already available at most general hospitals and will be supplied in all new district general hospitals. The major part of these services is provided on an out-patient basis; according to the OPCS Survey about 10% of the impaired living at home in Great Britain were receiving out-patient hospital treatment for their condition. There are also some rehabilitation centres which are not primarily associated with a particular hospital and which specialize in rehabilitation on an in-patient or out-patient basis. However, the provision of rehabilitation services has not in general adequately matched the changing pattern of disability and the problems were highlighted in the Tunbridge and Mair reports.[1]

As part of a programme to improve services, over £1 million has been allocated to provide some additional support for a number of existing centres which will demonstrate their expertise both locally and nationally, and eventually form the basis for a nation-wide network of first-class rehabilitation services.

Besides the general rehabilitation services, convalescence may be provided free of charge for all patients for whom a period of continued medical and nursing care is prescribed following treatment in hospital. Also, in most areas a speech therapy service is available for people handicapped with a speech or language impediment.

Treatment and rehabilitation services for the mentally ill and the mentally handicapped are provided at specialist psychiatric hospitals and, for the mentally ill, also at a small, but growing number of psychiatric units in general hospitals.

---

[1] *Rehabilitation.* Report of Sub-Committee (Chairman: Professor Sir Ronald Tunbridge) of the Standing Medical Advisory Committee, HMSO, 1972, £1. *Medical Rehabilitation: The Pattern for the Future.* Report of Sub-Committee (Chairman: Professor Alex Mair) of the Standing Medical Advisory Committee of the Scottish Health Services Council, HMSO, 1972.

General Practitioner (GP) Services

In the OPCS Survey, 37% of the impaired were in regular contact with their GP. For the handicapped, the Survey found that about 1 in 8 had regular consultations with their GP at least once every week and that more than 9 out of 10 had such consultations at least once every two months.

Drugs, etc., Aids and Appliances

Over 70% of the OPCS Survey sample used drugs because of their impairment, most of them on prescription.

An extensive range of aids and appliances is available. Each year a report[1] is made on progress in research and development work in relation to equipment that might increase the range of activities or well-being of handicapped people.

Invalid Vehicles

A description of the present arrangements for the supply of invalid vehicles, etc. under the National Health Service and the War Pensions scheme will be found in the Report on the Mobility of the Physically Disabled. The Report, due to be published in 1974, followed an independent inquiry into the mobility needs of the disabled which Lady Sharp carried out in 1972 and 1973. Lady Sharp's recommendations for future changes in the invalid vehicle service should be read in conjunction with Government statements on the Report.

Table A.7 indicates the extent of the help with transport which is given to National Health Service applicants and War Pensioners.

TABLE A.7 **Invalid vehicles, etc. on issue at 31.12.72.**

Type of Vehicle etc.	Numbers UK	Numbers England and Wales
Wheel chairs	156,105	142,260
Electric indoor chairs	3,125	3,017
Hand propelled tricycles	2,916	2,721
Powered invalid 3-wheelers	21,772	19,559
Motor cars	8,508	7,687
Private car maintenance allowances	10,877	10,091

[1] Research and Development Work on Equipment for the Disabled 1972. House of Commons Paper No. 299, HMSO, July 1973, 13p.

Local Authority Health and Personal Social Services

The Local Authority Social Services Act 1970 brought together the local authority welfare, mental health and children's services, which had formerly been administered separately, under one statutory social services committee and director of social services. The Act was passed at the same time as the Chronically Sick and Disabled Persons Act. The effect was to focus attention on the needs of the handicapped and to lead, both directly and indirectly, to a considerable expansion of services for them.

Section 1 of the Chronically Sick and Disabled Persons Act lays a duty on local authorities to inform themselves of the numbers and needs of 'substantially and permanently handicapped' people in their areas and to publicise their services to them; it refers back to Section 29 of the National Assistance Act 1948 which empowered local authorities to make arrangements for promoting the welfare of persons 'who are blind, deaf or dumb, and other persons who are substantially and permanently handicapped by illness, injury, or congenital deformity or such other disabilities as may be prescribed. . . .'

Section 2 of the Chronically Sick and Disabled Persons Act requires local authorities to make arrangements where in their view it is necessary for them to do so, to meet the needs of substantially and permanently handicapped people in a number of respects, including practical assistance in, and adaptations to the home; holidays and telephones.

Local authorities are under a duty to provide care and after care services for the mentally handicapped (and mentally ill) under Section 12 of the Health Services and Public Health Act 1968. These include centres for training and occupation, residential accommodation and social work and other supportive services. The present level of services available does not meet all needs and the 1971 White Paper[1] gave local authorities guidance on the levels of provision which they should aim to reach.

The range of services now provided by local social services authorities for people who are physically or mentally handicapped or who are, or have been mentally ill is wide.

Some services are provided in the home—health services such as health visiting and home nursing, and social services such as social work, home helps and meals on wheels. Examples of services provided outside the home include day care (including day nurseries), day centres of various kinds and occupational and recreational facilities. Residential

---

[1] Better Services for the Mentally Handicapped, Cmnd 4683, June 1971, HMSO, 45p. A White Paper on services for the mentally ill is due for publication in 1974.

services are also provided which may be needed either for short periods at times of special difficulty or on a permanent basis. There are, for example, hostels or homes for the physically handicapped, the mentally handicapped and the mentally ill. Of the 153,000 in residential accommodation for the elderly and physically handicapped in England and Wales on 31 March 1973, more than 140,000 were aged 65 or over.

Educational Needs of Handicapped Children

In November 1973, the Secretary of State for Education and Science announced that a committee was to be appointed 'to review educational provision in England, Scotland and Wales for children and young people handicapped by disabilities of body or mind, taking account of the medical aspects of their needs, together with arrangements to prepare them for entry into employment; to consider the most effective use of resources for these purposes; and to make recommendations'.

Employment Services

The Disabled Persons (Employment) Acts 1944 and 1958 form the basis of the employment services available to 'disabled' people. The 1944 Act defined a 'disabled' person as one who 'on account of injury, disease or congenital deformity, is substantially handicapped in obtaining or keeping employment, or in undertaking work on his own account, of a kind which apart from that injury, disease or deformity would be suited to his age, experience and qualifications'. Any person who comes within this definition and whose disability is likely to last at least 12 months may, under the Act, have his name entered on a register of disabled people, which may make it easier for him to obtain employment.

It is the responsibility of Disablement Resettlement Officers, most of whom are based on the larger employment offices, to advise disabled people on employment and to help them to gain employment. To assist disabled people to find employment the Disabled Persons (Employment) Act of 1944 imposes an obligation on all employers of 20 or more workers to employ a quota (at present 3%) of registered disabled people. The Secretary of State for Employment can also designate certain occupations to reserve further entry to them for registered disabled people. At present, designated occupations are restricted to two, namely, car park attendants and passenger electric lift attendants.

For those severely disabled people who require special supervision or, for example, who are too slow to work in normal surroundings, the Secretary of State for Employment can also provide 'sheltered employment'. Remploy Ltd is a non-profit making public company set up for that purpose. Local authorities and voluntary organizations also provide sheltered employment for severely disabled people.

The Disabled Persons (Employment) Acts also provide for courses in industrial rehabilitation to help disabled people to return to work. Certain private firms, in addition, have rehabilitation workshops for their employees. Vocational training of disabled people is conducted at Government training centres, at technical and commercial colleges, in open employment and at centres run by voluntary bodies.

The Department of Employment has been reviewing its existing specialized services for disabled people and preparing a series of consultative documents or discussion papers covering all its responsibilities in this field. A discussion paper on 'Resettlement Policy and Services for Disabled People' was issued in July 1972 and a consultative document on 'The Quota Scheme' was published in May 1973. A further consultative document, on Sheltered Employment, was due to be published at the end of 1973. The final topic to be covered was industrial rehabilitation and vocational training.

The following table (Table A.8) shows the expenditure in 1971–72 by the Department of Employment on the different parts of the employment services for the disabled. (HQ expenses concerned with determining policy are not included.)

TABLE A.8   **Expenditure by Department of Employment on Employment Services for Disabled People (Great Britain) 1971–72**

	Numbers dealt with in a year	Departmental Expenditure £ million	Cost per man assisted £
Placing Service:			
Placings of DPs by Department	59,595(a)	3·4	57
Industrial rehabilitation	11,675(b)	3·4(c)	291
Training	3,000(b)	3·4(c)	1,133
Sheltered employment	12,400(d)	7·6(e)	612

Notes:
(a) Rather more than this number place themselves.
(b) Complete courses.
(c) Inclusive of expenditure by all Government Departments.
(d) Average number of workers.
(e) Excludes all captal expenditure and estimated expenditure of £2·10m by local authoritiesi and £0·29m by voluntary bodies over and above the grants they receive from public funds.

Further Information

Further information about the benefits and services available to impaired and handicapped people can be obtained from the Government publications referred to in this Appendix and in the list below:

Department of Health and Social Security Annual Report 1972, Cmnd 5352, HMSO, 1973, £1.20. (Appendix III lists the Acts, Statutory Instruments, House of Commons Papers, Command Papers and other publications issued in 1972. It also lists over 100 explanatory leaflets which can be obtained free of charge from local offices of the Department.)

On the State of the Public Health. Annual Report of the Chief Medical Officer of the Department of Health and Social Security for 1972, HMSO, 1973, £1. (Includes chapters on 'Incapacity and Disablement', 'Mental Health and Social Handicap' and 'The Artificial Limb, Vehicle and Appliance Services'.)

Social Security Statistics 1972, HMSO, 1973, £2.25.

Health and Personal Social Services Statistics for England and Wales (with summary tables for Great Britain) 1972, HMSO, 1973, £1.85.

Department of Employment Services for Disabled Workers, Background Brief No. 5. Free from Information Branch, Department of Employment, 168 Regent Street, London W1R 5TB.

Appendix B
List of Conference Participants

Dr M. Agerholm	Queen Elizabeth's Foundation for the Disabled, Banstead
Dr R. L. Akehurst	Lancaster University
Professor E. M. Backett	Nottingham University
Mrs M. Blaxter	MRC Medical Sociology Unit, Aberdeen
Dr J. P. Bull	MRC Industrial Injuries and Burns Unit, Birmingham
Professor G. Calabresi	Yale University, USA
Dr P. J. Chapman	MRC, London
Mr A. J. Culyer	Institute of Economic and Social Research, York University
Professor R. O. Dalcq	Louvain University, Belgium
Dr R. F. F. Dawson	Transport and Road Research Laboratory, Crowthorne
Mr N. A. Doherty	Nottingham University
Mrs K. Dunnell	St Thomas's Hospital, London
Miss J. Garrad	Bristol University
Mr D. R. Harris	Centre for Socio-Legal Studies, Oxford
Dr K. Hawkins	Gonville and Caius College, Cambridge
Mrs V. Carstairs	Scottish Home and Health Department
Mr D. Hodgson	Law Commission, London
Mrs P. Jones	Centre for Applied Social Research, London
Dr A. Kushlick	Wessex Regional Hospital Board, Winchester
Professor D. S. Lees	Nottingham University
Professor R. C. O. Matthews	Chairman, SSRC, London
Mr H. McGregor	Wadham College, Oxford
Dr J. J. McMullen	General Practitioner, Chesham, Bucks.

Mr J. G. S. H. Mitchell	Secretary, SSRC, London
Mr G. Mooney	DHSS, London
Professor R. A. Parker	Bristol University
Mr D. Pole	DHSS, London
Mr M. Porter	Birmingham Accident Hospital
Mr J. H. Prevett	Bacon and Woodrow, Consulting Actuaries, London
Dr R. M. Rosser	The Maudsley Hospital, London
Dr P. Sainsbury	MRC Clinical Psychiatry Research Unit, Chichester
Miss S. Shaw	SSRC, London
Mr F. Sutton	DHSS, London
Mr G. Teeling-Smith	Office of Health Economics, London
Mr M. E. J. Wadsworth	MRC Unit on Environmental Factors in Mental and Physical Illness, London
Dr V. C. Watts	Arthur Andersen & Co, London
Professor A. Williams	York University